Freedom and Virtue

Freedom and Virtue

The Conservative/Libertarian Debate

Edited by George W. Carey

ISI Books

Wilmington, Delaware

Cataloging-in-Publication Data

Freedom and virtue: The conservative/libertarian debate/ edited
by George W. Carey. —Rev. ed. —Wilmington, Del. :   Intercollegiate Studies Institute, 1998.
           p.   cm.
           Includes bibliographical references.
ISBN   1-882926-96-X
           1. Libertarianism. 2. Conservatism. I. Carey, George Wescott,
1933-
JC585 .F74 1998   97-77876
320.51/2—dc21   CIP

Published in the United States by:

ISI Books
P.O. Box 4431
Wilmington, DE 19807-0431
www.isibooks.org

Manufactured in the United States of America

Contents

Acknowledgments

The editor wishes to acknowledge that permissions have been granted for the reprinting of the following essays:

"Do-It-Yourself Conservatism?," M. Morton Auerbach vs. M. Stanton Evans, Frank S. Meyer, and Russell Kirk, appeared first in the January 30, 1962 issue of *National Review*.

"The Twisted Tree of Liberty" by Frank S. Meyer was first published in the January 16, 1962 edition of *National Review*.

"Freedom or Virtue?" by L. Brent Bozell first appeared in *National Review* on September 1, 1962.

"Conservatism and Libertarianism" by Richard M. Weaver was originally published in the May 1960 issue of *The Individualist*.

"Freedom and Virtue: Allies or Antagonists?" and "Love *versus* Freedom" originally appeared in the Spring 1995 issue of the *Intercollegiate Review* as "Freedom or Virtue? An Exchange" between Doug Bandow and Frederick D. Wilhelmsen, respectively.

The following essays have been abridged for this edition: "Conservatism and Libertarianism: Vital Complements" by John P. East; "Differences of Theory and Strategy" by John Hospers; "Libertarianism as the Philosophy of Moral Freedom: A Response" by Edward B. McLean.

"A Dispassionate Assessment of Libertarians" by Russell Kirk replaces his essay, "Libertarians: The Chirping Sectaries." This essay first appeared in his book, *The Politics of Prudence* (Bryn Mawr: Intercollegiate Studies Institute, Inc., 1993).

Introduction

GEORGE W. CAREY

The reception accorded the first edition of these essays clearly indicates a widespread and intense concern about the relationship between freedom and virtue. While, to be sure, this relationship is interesting to thoughtful students of virtually every political persuasion, it is of special importance for American conservatives and libertarians because it has been, and continues to be, a source of great controversy. At the philosophical level, at least, it serves to divide the conservative/libertarian alliance that has long resisted the growth of the liberal welfare state. As liberalism wanes and public policy formation is increasingly driven by conservative and libertarian values, this schism promises to become even wider.

In its broadest terms, the freedom/virtue debate can be understood as arising from the primacy accorded individual liberty in libertarian thought. Libertarians, as certain of the following essays will make abundantly clear, share John Stuart Mill's view concerning "the nature and limits of the power which can be legitimately exercised by society over the individual";[1] namely, "the sole end for which mankind are warranted, individually or collectively, in interfering with the liberty of action of any of their number is self-protection."[2] In his introductory chapter to *On Liberty,* Mill forcefully advances this position. He maintains that this "one very simple principle" should "govern absolutely the dealings of society with the individual in the way of compulsion and control, whether the means used by physical force in the form of legal penalties, or the moral coercion of public opinion."[3] "The only purpose," he contends, "for which power can be rightfully exercised over any member of a civilized community, against his will, is to prevent harm to others."[4] Even the individual's "own good, either physical or moral," he argues, "is not a sufficient warrant" for interfering with his liberty.[5] On this score, he writes, conduct "which merely concerns himself, his independence is, of right, absolute. Over himself, over his own body and mind, the individual is sovereign."[6]

These principles, we should note, far from being lofty and abstract precepts, formed the basis for what is known as "classical liberalism" that flourished in England and the United States during the late nineteenth and early twentieth centuries. The goal of classical liberalism is the maximization of individual liberty in both the political and economic spheres. Unlike contemporary American liberals or progressives, classical liberals resist governmental rules and regulations, holding that individual liberty is best served by minimal government.

The vast majority of conservatives—certainly the traditionalists or "paleoconservatives," but also the "neoconservatives"—while concerned with individual liberty, strongly believe that shared values, morals, and standards, along with accepted traditions, are necessary for the order and stability of society; that, moreover, without these socially cohesive elements, the environment necessary for the moral and intellectual development of individuals is seriously lacking. They stress as well the need for virtue, a problem particularly acute in republican regimes where the people ultimately rule. They would agree with the point made by James Madison in an oft-quoted passage at the conclusion of Federalist paper essay 55; namely, a "Republican government presupposes the existence of" the benign "qualities" of human nature "in a higher degree than any other form."[7]

Conservatives have long accepted the teachings of the classics that underscore the need for regimes to cultivate and perpetuate the virtues appropriate for their character, if they are to endure. But we do not have to bring the classics to bear to understand the concerns of modern conservatives in this regard. As those familiar with the American tradition know, a concern with the virtues necessary for a republican regime arises at various points in our political tradition, particularly during the formative years of the republic. And, to a surprising degree, the views and concerns of the commentators of this period reflect those of contemporary American conservatism. Jeremiah Atwater, for instance, acknowledging that the United States at that time (1801) enjoyed a "mild and free government," proceeds to ask: "to what is this owing?" "Is it," he asks rhetorically, "that man needs no restraint; but will, unless made vicious by government, always act as a reasonable being, and be obedient and virtuous, because it is his highest interest to be so?" Atwater observes that this answer is based upon a "theoretical idea" that embodies a false understanding of human nature. As he would have it, the virtuous citizen is formed by restraints, not unrestricted liberty. "Man," he writes, "from cradle to grave, is constantly learning new lessons of moral instruction, and is trained to virtue and order by perpetual and salutary restraints"; restraints imposed by the family, by the schools, by government and laws, and even by "public opinion, which, in a country where Christianity is believed, compels even profligates to be outwardly virtuous."[8]

Like most modern conservatives, many of the religious and civil leaders of this earlier period believed that an aspect of the public virtue consisted in shared values and a common morality that would, in the words of Zephaniah Swift Moore (the first president of Amherst College), provide a "uniform direction of the public will to that which is good."[9] Closely connected to this belief was another which finds strong support among conservatives today, namely, that the source of this morality, as Samuel Kendal declared, must have "some higher origin than the consent of the political bodies." "Nothing is gained," Kendal held, if the laws of morality "are not supposed to proceed from some superior power, to which human beings are amenable."[10] For him, "the imperfection of man" is such "that nothing depending on human authority only is adequate to the proposed end of civil government." Thus, he reasoned, "Religious faith, or sentiment, must...be called in to the support of that morality, which is essential to the order and well-being of society."[11]

These concerns and observations, aside from embodying enduring elements of conservative belief, point to the underlying reasons why many contemporary conservatives believe that we are facing a social crisis of perhaps unprecedented proportions. These conservatives believe that the damage to the fabric and cohesiveness of society due to the loss of virtue and a common morality, is even more devastating than that anticipated by Atwater, Moore, Kendal, and others.

A host of works, far too numerous to deal with here, have concentrated on one or more aspects of this social degeneration. Most seem to be in agreement that the down hill slide began to accelerate at an alarming rate sometime in the late 1960's. Many of these critics would accept the scenario painted by the *Wall Street Journal* in a particularly hard-hitting editorial, "No Guardrails," that places the beginning of our precipitous decline in August 1968, "when the Democratic National Convention found itself sharing Chicago with the street fighters of the anti-Vietnam War movement." Absolving the protectors from responsibility for what followed, the editorial focuses on "university professors, politicians and journalistic commentators— who said then that the acts committed by the protesters were justified or explainable," thereby absolving the protesters from responsibility for what followed. "With great rhetorical firepower," the editorial notes, "books, magazines, opinion columns and editorials defended each succeeding act of defiance—against the war, against university presidents, against corporate practices, against behavior codes, against dress codes, against virtually all agents of established authority."[12] The editorial laments that the "guardrails"—that is, the rules that provide the framework for acceptable behavior within society—were also a casualty of this movement.

Conservatives are also in substantial agreement concerning what Anthony Harrigan terms "the major components of the decadence" that have overtaken American society. One of the major components, Harrigan insists, are "those in the entertainment business who have profited from contributing to the collapse of the established moral order." He regards these individuals to be "among the most pernicious enemies of our society, corrupters of a generation" who have "engaged in deliberate destruction of essential codes and conventions that ensured civilized life in this country."[13] Robert Bork, in his appropriately titled book, *Slouching Towards Gomorrah*, notes the prevalence of lewdness, vulgarity, and obscenity in our popular culture that he believes has "brutalized" our society and undermined our standards of decency. Noting that John Stuart Mill "himself would be horrified at what we have become," Bork seriously considers whether censorship of movies, television, recordings and reading materials might serve as a remedy. Unlike many contemporary liberals and libertarians, Bork insists, Mill did not intend his "one very simple principle" to be used as a justification for an unrestrained popular culture that produces and sustains a violent and degenerate society.[14] William Bennett has constructed "An Index of Leading Cultural Indicators" to offer a quantitative picture of our cultural decline. Since the 1960's he finds "a 560 percent increase in violent crime," over "a 400 percent increase in illegitimate births," and more than three times as many "children living in single parent homes." In 1940, he writes, "talking out of turn; chewing gum; making noise; running in the halls; cutting in line; dress code infractions; and littering" were identified by teachers as the leading problems in the public schools. In the 1990's these problems were replaced by "drug abuse; alcohol; pregnancy; suicide; rape; robbery; and assault."[15] In sum, to go no further, conservatives, now as perhaps never before, are alarmed at the consequences of what they perceive to be the abandonment of moral standards, mores, and traditions, along with the almost total erosion of both public and private virtues.

Now most libertarians are alarmed at the state of affairs as well. They would, however, take exception with conservatives over its causes and solutions. They would acknowledge, most at any rate, that our present social conditions are at least in part due to liberty that has been used badly. Nevertheless, many would argue, liberty is too precious a commodity to be regulated and controlled in the fashion that conservatives would seem to favor, e.g., through education in virtue, obedience to moral codes, mores, and traditions, or censorship. Rather, they would emphasize that blind conformity to a moral or religious code does not constitute virtuous behavior nor does it make individuals more virtuous; that, on the contrary, liberty or freedom is a necessary condition for choice and that choice, in turn, is a necessary condition for the practice, realization, and cultivation of virtue. Aside from this, in the words of Friedrich von Hayek, libertarians have "an intellectual commitment to a type of order in which, even on issues which to one are fundamental, others are allowed to pursue different ends." Writing from the perspective of a classical liberal, he continues, "It is for this reason that to the [classical] liberal neither moral nor religious ideals are proper objects of coercion." "The view that moral beliefs concerning matters of conduct which do not directly interfere with the protected sphere of other persons do not justify coercion," he feels, may be "the most conspicuous attribute of [classical] liberalism that distinguishes it as much from conservatism as from socialism."[16]

A basic libertarian argument on behalf of liberty is not unlike that set forth by Madison in Federalist paper 10 in his discussion of the relationship between factions and liberty. Madison acknowledges that liberty is necessary for the formation of factions, which he defines as a "number of citizens...who are united and actuated by some common impulse of passion, or of interest, adverse to the rights of other citizens, or to the permanent and aggregate interests of the community."[17] Factions he regarded to be potentially fatal "diseases most incident to Republican Government."[18] Yet, he concludes that the "remedy," "destroying the liberty which is essential to" the "existence" of factions, would be "worse than the disease." "Liberty is to faction," he writes, "what air is to fire, an aliment without which it instantly expires. But it could not be less folly to abolish liberty, which is essential to political life, because it nourishes faction, than it would be to wish the annihilation of air, which is essential to animal life, because it imparts to the fire its destructive agency."[19] This view, which places a very high premium on liberty, comports with the stance taken by libertarians when confronted with the abuses of liberty that have caused the social deterioration which conservatives and others deplore.

The foregoing presents only in broad outline the character and dimensions of the division between libertarians and conservatives. The following essays will reveal the character and nuances of these differences, as well as other sources of division. But this should not blind us to the areas of agreement, which if nothing else, have served to unite the two schools at the level of practical politics, particularly in their opposition to the centralized, welfare state and those policies that would enlarge its powers.

The collapse of the Soviet Union may have served to provide even a stronger union between these schools regarding the powers of government in both the national and international arenas. Whereas virtually all conservatives during the Cold War period were strongly anti-communist and, accordingly, supported a strong national government with the powers necessary to combat communism both internally and externally, many libertarians felt the Soviet threat was vastly exaggerated, primarily as a cover to expand the powers of government. While conservatives were prone to regard the Cold War confrontations with the Soviet Union as part of a larger conflict involving the survival of the better part of Western civilization, it was something far less than this for certain libertarians. Currently, in the absence of a credible threat to the survival of our nation, some schools of conservative thought can be expected to join libertarians in opposing interventionist foreign policies and any expansion of the powers of the national government, particularly with respect to monitoring and policing domestic groups.

Because of their close association in the arena of practical politics, the question has arisen whether there are

philosophical grounds on which conservatives and libertarians can merge or "fuse." Is it possible, that is, to
reconcile the libertarian concern for individual liberty with
the conservatives' preoccupation with order and virtue? Or
are the differences so fundamental that the two schools can
never be joined at the theoretical level? Though these
questions had been simmering beneath the surface for
some time among the intellectual leaders of the post World
War II conservative movement, particularly among those
who had united with William Buckley in 1955 to launch
National Review, they did not come into full public view
until January 1962 with the publication of an article in
National Review by Professor M. Morton Auerbach entitled "Do-It-Yourself Conservatism?" At the urging of
William Buckley, three leading conservatives—M. Stanton
Evans, Frank S. Meyer, and Russell Kirk—responded to
Auerbach's critique of modern conservatism. In turn, their
responses were examined critically some months later in a
lengthy article, "Freedom or Virtue?," by L. Brent Bozell
that also appeared in *National Review*. In many ways, the
ensuing arguments over the years concerning the relationship between libertarianism and conservatism are extended
footnotes to points made in these early exchanges. For that
reason, we have placed them at the beginning of this
collection.

    That the leaders of post World War II conservatism were
aware of the potential split in the conservative movement
over the freedom/virtue issue before the matter was aired
publicly is attested to by the publication of Frank S. Meyer's
In Defense of Freedom in 1962, soon after the appearance of
Auerbach's article.[20] In this work, Meyer set forth what has

come to be known as "fusionism," namely, the position that the theoretical differences could be reconciled given the proper social and political environment. From his perspective such an environment was one whose social and political ethos would allow individuals to "freely choose" and whose "intellectual and moral leaders, the 'creative minority,'" possessed the requisite "understanding and imagination to maintain the prestige of tradition and reason" to "sustain the intellectual and moral order throughout society."[21] This "simultaneous belief in objectively existing moral value and in the freedom of the individual person," he believed, was rooted in the Declaration of Independence and the Constitution, as it was understood at the time of adoption. From his vantage point, it represented as well the "consensus of contemporary conservatism."[22] In sum, then, Meyer's fusionism consisted of a wide range of individual liberty to choose (the paramount libertarian value) within an order that embodied reason and tradition (a condition that takes into account traditional conservative concerns).

Meyer's fusionism provides a convenient point of reference for understanding the various positions set forth concerning the relationship between libertarianism and conservatism in the essays that follow. Many of these essays, whether specifically addressing Meyer's formulation or not, deal with the question of whether there can be theoretical union between conservatives, who place a high value on tradition, order, and virtue, and libertarians, who accord primacy to individual liberty. Other essays deal directly with the question of whether Meyer's argument is sound; whether, that is, he satisfactorily makes the case for his fusionism. I will not even try to canvass the varied questions and concerns raised in these essays because I think it best that the readers confront them first hand.

I have made certain significant changes from the first edition of this work, all intended to shed more light on the freedom/virtue controversy. To the essays that appeared in the first edition[23] I have added "Do-It-Yourself Conservatism?" (*National Review*, 30 January 1962) which contains the article by M. Morton Auerbach and the responses by M. Stanton Evans, Frank S. Meyer, and Russell Kirk; "The Twisted Tree of Liberty" (*National Review*, 16 January 1962) by Frank S. Meyer and, in slightly abridged form, "Freedom or Virtue?" from L. Brent Bozell (*National Review*, 1 September 1962). As noted above these essays provide a highly useful background for understanding the subsequent debates over liberty and virtue.

I have also added a short essay by Richard Weaver, "Conservatism and Libertarianism" (*The Individualist*, May 1960); and the exchange, "Freedom or Virtue?" between Doug Bandow and Frederick D. Wilhelmsen (*Intercollegiate Review*, Spring 1995).

Finally, I have replaced Russell Kirk's "Libertarians: The Chirping Sectaries" with his "A Dispassionate Assessment of Libertarians" from *The Politics of Prudence* (Bryn Mawr: Intercollegiate Studies Institute, 1993).

Notes

1. *Utilitarianism, Liberty and Representative Government* (New York: Precepts, 1950), 85.
2. *Ibid.*, 95.
3. *Ibid.*
4. *Ibid.*, 95-96.

5. *Ibid.*
6. *Ibid.*
7. Hamilton, Madison, and Jay, *The Federalist*, George W. Carey and James McClellan, eds. (Dubuque, Iowa: Kendall/Hunt, 1990), 289. All references to The Federalist are to this edition.
8. *American Political Writing during the Founding Era, 1760-1805,* Charles S. Hyneman and Donald S. Lutz, eds. 2 Vols. (Indianapolis: Liberty Press, 1983), II, 1177.
9. *Ibid.*, II, 1213.
10. *Ibid.*, II, 1245.
11. *Ibid.*, II, 1244.
12. "No Guardrails," in "Review & Outlook," *Wall Street Journal*, 18 March 1993, A12.
13. Anthony Harrigan, "A Lost Civilization," *Modern Age* (Fall 1992), 6-7.
14. Robert H. Bork, *Slouching Towards Gomorrah: Modern Liberalism and American Decline* (New York: HarperCollins, 1996), 153.
15. William J. Bennett, *The Index of Leading Cultural Indicators* (Washington, D. C., 1993), xxi. This study was jointly published by the Heritage Foundation and Empower America.
16. F. A. Hayek, *The Constitution of Liberty* (Chicago: University of Chicago Press, 1960), 402. These remarks appear in his "Postscript" entitled "Why I Am Not a Conservative."
17. *The Federalist*, 43-44.
18. *Ibid.*, 48.
19. *Ibid.*, 44.
20. The best account of the post-World War II Conservative Movement through the early 1970's is George H. Nash's, *The Conservative Intellectual Movement in America: Since 1945* first published in 1976. This valuable work was republished in 1996 by the Intercollegiate Studies Institute with an Epilogue by the author.
21. Frank S. Meyer, *In Defense of Freedom* (Chicago: Henry Regnery Company, 1962), 69.
22. *Ibid.*, 5.
23. The essays by Robert Nisbet, Walter Berns, John East, and Tibor Machan appeared as articles in *Modern Age* 24 (Winter 1980). These articles were revised versions of papers presented at the Chicago meeting of the Philadelphia Society in April 1979. The essays by Murray Rothbard, M.

Stanton Evans, and John Hospers were originally papers presented at a Liberty Fund conference on fusionism at Pompano Beach, Florida in January 1981. These papers were published in *Modern Age* 26 (Spring 1982). Edward McLean's response to the Kurtz article was specially written for this volume.

Do-It-Yourself Conservatism?*

M. MORTON AUERBACH
(VS. M. STANTON EVANS,
FRANK S. MEYER, AND RUSSELL KIRK)

Anyone who has tried to apply the term "conservative" to more than one period of history knows that the word is extremely flexible. In its original eighteenth-century European usage, "conservative" referred to an opponent of the French Revolution. The tradition against which the Revolution was directed was the heritage of the Middle Ages. Therefore, a conservative was at that time one who defended medieval values against the "liberals" who supported the principles of revolutionary France. Among other things, the conservative medievalists believed in the supreme importance of 1) a cohesive, organic community; 2) a code of "natural law" and religious orthodoxy which emphasizes moral obligations and duties; 3) a sharply graded system of social status which teaches each to stay in his "allotted place" in society; 4) a citizenry which demands no more of the community than what custom assigns to one's social position; and 5) leadership at the top by a

*This essay appears as it did in the January 30, 1962 issue of *National Review*.

leisured aristocracy. The liberal revolutionaries denied the primacy of every one of these concepts. Their ideology favored 1) the individual instead of the community; 2) a moral code which began with "natural rights" and freedoms instead of duties; 3) a society based on open competition instead of social status; 4) a citizenry which expects reward according to individual ability instead of custom; and 5) leadership by the middle class. These premises led liberals to conclude that a good society should have free enterprise, civil liberties, and limited government.

For twentieth-century Americans the terms "conservative" and "liberal" have acquired not only different meanings but self-contradictory ones. *National Review* now calls someone a Liberal if he favors the administrative or the welfare state, regardless of whether he does so for socialist reasons, for authoritarian reasons, or for reasons which are still liberal in the original sense of the word. On the other hand, we usually use the word "conservative" to mean one who wants government to leave private enterprise alone. In other words, what was once liberalism has now become conservatism. To increase the confusion, a number of intellectuals (who are called the "new conservatives") have been trying recently to link American conservatism to Edmund Burke, the classic spokesman for the original medieval form of conservatism. Consequently, the term "conservatism" is now being used to mean opposition to the administrative state, regardless of whether the opposition results from classical liberal or from medieval premises. Thus, Barry Goldwater, obviously a conservative of the classical liberal variety, cites Russell Kirk as his favorite theoretician, in spite of the fact that Kirk is an avowed Burkean who deplores the passing of aristocracy. Frederick

Wilhelmsen, whose favorite period of history seems to lie somewhere in the Middle Ages, appears alongside William Buckley, whose preference would almost certainly be for one or more of the liberal centuries. And Russell Kirk, who has charged Buckley with erroneous defense of individualism, continues to be a favorite of Buckley's *National Review*.

The fallacious attempt to link medievalism with classical liberalism goes back to Burke himself who, unlike Continental conservatives of the eighteenth century, wanted to defend a version of medievalism which was tempered by a considerable amount of liberalism. Some months ago, in a book entitled *The Conservative Illusion*, I discussed the many contradictions to which Burke was forced because of his insistence on keeping both medievalism and liberalism in a single political theory. I also demonstrated that Burke's followers (the "new conservatives") have simply built new contradictions on his old ones, without ever having resolved the original problem.

The Conservative Illusion dealt exclusively with the predominantly medieval, Burkean type of conservatism and *not at all* with the primarily liberal type of conservatism to be found in *National Review*. The response of *National Review* [M. Stanton Evans' review, Jan. 30, 1960] provided a fascinating study in evasion. First it charged that my analysis of Burke was a "verbal agony," the charge apparently resting on the premise that if I found any contradictions in Burke, it must be my fault, not his. Then it dismissed the rest of the book on the grounds that it was not directed at "authentic" conservatism. "Authentic" conservatism turned out to be primarily the classical liberalism of

James Madison, which was simply not the subject of the book. But the list of authentics simultaneously included Burkeans and others whose first premises are medieval. Thus the review concluded with precisely the fallacy which it found so inconceivable in my analysis of Burke.

Consider the position of William Buckley. Even from a casual reading of his books, one can see that his major premises rest primarily on the desire to maximize individual freedom and competition. Like most American conservatives, Buckley is interested first in increasing economic freedom by diminishing the economic role of government. But a preponderance of both educators and voters have been willing to maintain and probably increase government participation in economics. Therefore, to allow intellectual and political freedom under present conditions is to allow increasing restrictions on economic freedom. Conversely, one who would affirm this last freedom must restrict the first two. One of Buckley's major arguments against what he calls "Liberals" is that in choosing to follow intellectual freedom and political democracy wherever they may lead, the "Liberals" have been destroying economic freedom, thus being guilty of a major inconsistency. But if this is wrong, then why is it valid for Buckley simply to turn the fallacy upside down? If freedom is the supreme value, then isn't the diminution of any freedom wrong, whether economic, intellectual, or political?

It follows that Buckley would have a much more difficult time justifying all of his positions if he had to do so with the same premise, namely, the need to maximize individual freedom. It is much easier simply to tailor the argument to the occasion. Thus, when he wants a clear statement of the limits on legitimate government intervention in private affairs he turns to an early formulation of John Stuart Mill or some classical liberal formulation. But when he wants to argue for intellectual conformity to "tradition," Buckley suddenly begins quoting from Edmund Burke conveniently glossing over the fact that he uses "tradition" to mean specifically the classical liberal tradition, while Burke uses the word to mean primarily the medieval tradition. Indeed, Burkean arguments are always handy when Buckley needs to avoid embarrassing responsibility to the concept of freedom, even though he never uses Burke's terminology in its original meaning. Could this be why it has become so important for *National Review* to maintain an imaginary escape tunnel connecting Burke with James Madison, i.e., joining medievalism and classical liberalism? Will conservatism continue to offer nothing more than an array of mutually exclusive "principles" from which all are invited to pick what suits them? Is this the age of do-it-yourself conservatism?

Techniques and Circumstances
M. Stanton Evans

Mr. Auerbach's problem, I think, is twofold: First, he obviously does identify his subject with "medievalism," repeatedly defining conservatism as the amalgam of convictions, techniques and moods which marked the politics of an aristocratic past. He fails to determine which elements in that amalgam are essential points of philosophy, and which are technical or stylistic epiphenomena characterizing it at a particular point in time. Thus, in his present list of conservative beliefs, he makes no apparent distinction between "a code of natural law" and "leadership at the top of a leisured aristocracy." He ignores the truism that while principles are by definition constant, the technique by which they can be vindicated may alter from age—e.g., when understanding is improved by experience or new information (as Hamilton suggested in Federalist No. 9), or when circumstances have become changed so radically that former techniques are no longer effective (as when liberalism, not conservatism, has become the *status quo*).

Second, having failed to isolate the essentials of conservative philosophy, Auerbach inevitably fails to demonstrate any system of relations between that philosophy and the form of our political institutions. He therefore fails to demonstrate a necessary disjunction between conservative principles and political liberty, and thus to prove his asserted "inconsistency" on the part of libertarian conservatives.

If we view conservatism as a philosophy, rather than as an immutable catalogue of tastes and foibles, I think we can attribute to it certain primary and constant affirmations. The conservative believes ours is a God-centered, and therefore an ordered, universe; that man's purpose is to shape his life to the patterns of order proceeding from the Divine center of life; and that, in seeking this objective, man is hampered by a fallible intellect and vagrant will.

Properly construed, this view of things is not only compatible with a due regard for human freedom, but demands it.

The conservative's first concern is that man restrain his appetites by the imperatives of right choice—choice which can take place only in circumstances favoring volition. Moreover, the reign of appetite is most destructive, and the incentives and opportunities for its exercise most plentiful, when fallible man is endowed with unlimited power over his fellow beings. If man is corrupted in mind and impulse, he is hardly to be trusted with the unbridled potencies of the state. For both reasons, the limitation of government power becomes the highest *political* objective of conservatism.

That conservative views on the nature of man are commensurable with political liberty is demonstrated by the American Constitution. Mr. Auerbach's flinging about of the phrase "classical liberalism" cannot alter the fact that the Constitution, premised upon a deep mistrust of human nature and designed to curb its excesses, is a profoundly conservative document. A canvas of the debates in convention, and of the commentaries of Madison, reveals our Constitution-makers anxious to maintain freedom by counterpoising ambitions and placing countless impediments in the way of change; and to a large extent, their work was successful. What Mr. Auerbach calls an "inconsistency" is in fact the vital equilibrium, centered in the wisdom of conservatism, of the free society.

By protesting that these are not the sort of people about whom he was writing, Mr. Auerbach destroys his original effort to prove conservatism an "illusion" incapable of practical results. Indeed, if he confesses that he excludes the conservative movement as it now exists in the United States, it becomes apparent that it is Mr. Auerbach's book, and not conservatism, which is irrelevant to reality.

The Separation of Powers

Frank S. Meyer

In his reply to Stanton Evans' review of *The Conservative Illusion*, Professor Auerbach restates more succinctly the central contentions of the book itself: 1) that a belief in transcendental truth is incompatible with a belief in individual human freedom, and 2) that therefore the rapidly growing American conservatism of today is an intellectual monstrosity rent by contradictions.

What Professor Auerbach fails to understand is that the Christian understanding of the nature and destiny of man, which is the foundation of Western civilization, is always and everywhere what conservatives strive to conserve. That understanding accepts the existence of absolute truth and good and at the same time recognizes that men are created with the free will to accept or reject that truth and good. Conservatism, therefore, demands both the struggle to vindicate truth and good and the establishment of conditions in which the free will of individual persons can be effectively exercised.

Conservatism sees two overriding evils in society. On the one hand, it fights against determinist philosophies, which equate truth and good with whatever happens historically to succeed, and against relativist philosophies, which deny the very existence of truth and good. On the other hand, it resists the growth of a monopoly of power, usually exercised through the state, which suppresses or distorts the exercise of free will by individual persons. It believes, further, that such a monopoly of force can be as thoroughly and evilly exercised by a "democratic" majority as by an "aristocratic" minority or by a single tyrant. Professor Auerbach is right when he says that conservatives oppose the contemporary aggrandizement of the state and its movement towards totalitarianism (what he so gently characterizes as "the administrative state"), for the aggrandizing state is the enemy of the freedom of the person. He is wrong when he regards such opposition as incompatible with "medieval" belief in "natural law and religious orthodoxy." Indeed, the Middle Ages maintained a separation of powers both through the geographically decentralized institutions of feudalism and through the balance of powers between church and state. That separation of powers placed feudal Europe, as Professor Wittfogel has demonstrated in his *Oriental Despotism*, among the freest societies in the history of man.

American conservatives do not wish to return to medieval conditions. They do wish, in modern conditions, to preserve and develop the tension between the transcendent ends of man and the freedom through which he can attain those ends, the tension which Western civilization has always expressed. They will not be diverted from pursuing that course by semantic or historicist arguments based upon the struggles between nineteenth-century conservatives and nineteenth-century liberals. The nineteenth century, heir to the disruption of the French Revolution, was a brief and distorted era in the long history of Western civilization. In its struggles there was truth on both sides, and from both sides the contemporary American conservative can learn. But it is the authentic tradition of the West which he is striving to recover, a tradition which goes far deeper than the parochial disputes of the nineteenth century.

The American conservative has indeed a special heritage, the discussions and the achievements of the Founders of the American Constitution (Madison pre-eminently), men who established the highest political form the West has yet created to express the tension of transcendent truth and human freedom. The political structure they left us has its contradictions, no doubt; but, like the contradictions Professor Auerbach finds among American conservatives today, they reflect the imperfect state of man and the tension within which he must live if he is to be true to his nature, striving towards transcendent ends in freedom.

Conservatism Is Not an Ideology
Russell Kirk

Mr. Auerbach's fundamental difficulties are two:

1) He thinks of political preferences as rigid categories, or compartments, made up of abstractions relentlessly adhered to, regardless of altered circumstances: in short, he confounds political theory with ideology. Since conservatism never was an ideology, he is all adrift.

2) He thinks of political ideas as somehow bound to neat historical periods—"medieval," "nineteenth century," and

the like. In truth, great political ideas transcend particular institutions and periods. The reflecting conservative adheres not to some idealized historical era, but to what Dr. Leo Strauss calls "the Great Tradition."

This confusion leads Mr. Auerbach into his errors about Burke. What Burke championed was not "medievalism," but the Great Tradition. He was defending the politics of Cicero, the moral system of Christianity, and the civil social order which had developed so successfully in England. (That Mr. Auerbach can think of England in the latter half of the eighteenth century as somehow medieval serves to justify Jacques Barzun's strictures on the American Ph.D.; a cursory reading of Lecky or Leslie Stephen would have dispelled this curious illusion.) There is no inconsistency between the *Letter to a Noble Lord* and *Thoughts on Scarcity*: for Burke was not trying to harmonize medieval economic practices and constitutional government, but rather was engaged in a justification of certain enduring moral and political norms.

Similarly, Auerbach seems to think that Burke's defense of aristocracy is somehow medieval—and that therefore Senator Goldwater cannot hold the same concept of just leadership. (According to this line of reasoning, John Adams, too, must have been a medievalist—and even Jefferson.) But what Burke actually said is this: "A true natural aristocracy is not a separate interest in the state, or separable from it. It is an essential integrant part of any large body rightly constituted. It is formed out of a class of legitimate presumptions, which, taken as generalities, must be admitted for actual truths." And Burke goes on to include among this natural aristocracy—not merely landed proprietors, but the genuinely leisured and strictly educated; the administrators of law and justice; professors of science and arts; rich traders with their "habitual regard to commutative justice." One remarkable good expression of this natural aristocracy, as things have turned out, is the United States Senate, of which Mr. Barry Goldwater is so eminent a member. Such an aristocracy is not "medieval," but simply essential to every just and successful civil social order.

Mr. Auerbach, a liberal ideologue, is distressed because conservatives are making headway nowadays—and so he reproaches them for not behaving like ideologues of another persuasion. But I fear that thinking conservatives will not meekly squeeze themselves into Mr. Auerbach's rather medieval categories. What we have seen during recent years in this country, and somewhat earlier in Britain, is the gradual fusion of conservatives and old-fangled liberals (the minority faction of the liberal interest) into a fairly coherent body of opinion. Walter Bagehot predicted, and approved, this development as early as 1875. Not being ideologues, people of conservative convictions have modified and improved their practical politics to suit the needs of our age. But being ideologues, liberals of Mr. Auerbach's stamp cling to hollow slogans, refusing to admit that liberalism is a dead thing in the twentieth century: and thus we arrive at the paradox which Mr. Auerbach cannot see, that nowadays liberals are far more mossbacked, and "conservative" in the bad sense of the term—an inverted conservatism of negations—than are the real conservatives.

The Twisted Tree
of Liberty*

FRANK S. MEYER

In the spectrum of American Conservatism there are and
have been many different groupings, holding varying positions within the same broad outlook. Some have emphasized the menace of international Communism; others
have emphasized the danger of the creeping rot at the heart
of our own institutions. Some stress the corrosion of
tradition, and with it of the natural law of justice, as the
source of our afflictions; others, an intellectual failure to
grasp the prime importance of freedom in the body politic.
Nevertheless, whatever the differences in emphasis, there
has been general agreement in the practical political sphere
on the necessity both to resist the collectivism and statism
that emanates from indigenous Liberalism and simultaneously to repel and overcome the Communist attack
upon Western civilization, which—though it has its sub-
versive detachments operating domestically—is primarily

*This essay appears as it did in the January 16, 1962 issue of
National Review.

based upon the armed power of a foreign enemy.

There have been, of course, tendencies to overstress one aspect or another to such a degree that those who do so tend to move right out of the spectrum. There have been some who concentrate so wholeheartedly on the menace of domestic Communism that its international character is lost sight of and the true role of Liberalism is only cloudily understood. There have been some with such concern for the deterioration of the philosophical foundations of virtue and justice that they neglect almost totally the corollary—that in the political realm freedom is the pre-condition of a good society. But whatever strains these one-sided emphases have created in the growth towards a mature political and philosophical American conservative position, there has not been until lately any grouping which directly and explicitly opposes itself to the defense of freedom from either its domestic or foreign enemies.

Recently, however, there has arisen for the first time a considered position, developed out of the "pure libertarian" sector of right-wing opinion, which sharply repudiates the struggle against the major and most immediate contemporary enemy of freedom, Soviet Communism—and does so on grounds, purportedly, of a love for freedom. These "pure libertarian" pacifists applaud Krushchev, support the Fair Play for Cuba Committee, join the Sane Nuclear Policy Committee, and toy with the tactic of a united front with Communists "against war." They project themselves as the true representatives of the Right, attacking the militantly anti-Communist position of the leadership of American conservatism as moving towards the destruction of individual liberty because it is prepared to

use the power of the American state in one of its legitimate
functions, to defend freedom against Communist totalitarianism.

It might seem that there is no point to discussing a view of
reality so patently distorted that it can consider appeasement of Communism, disarming ourselves before the
Communist armed drive and alliance with those who ease
the road to Communist victory, as essential to the defense
of freedom of the individual. But although those who
profess these absurd opinions are small in number, they do
influence a section of the right wing, particularly in the
universities, and they may, if not combated, influence
more, for they offer tempting fleshpots: the opportunity to
proclaim devotion to individual freedom, championship of
the free-market economy, and opposition to prevailing
Liberal welfare-statism, while comfortably basking in the
sunshine of the Liberal atmosphere, which is today primarily the atmosphere of appeasement and piecemeal surren-
der.

Shocking though they are, the practical results of this
pacifist strain in the right wing are minimal; more important is the light that the development of such monstrous
misapprehension of reality casts upon the dangers inherent in the "pure libertarian" approach to the problems of
freedom in society. It is a tendency which, followed unchecked, can be as harmful to the development of a mature
American conservative position as the counter-tendency
in the conservative penumbra—concerning which I have
written previously in these pages—to look upon the state

as unlimitedly instituted to enforce virtue, thus abnegating the freedom of the individual.

Of course, in any healthy growing movement there are bound to be clashes of opinion, differences of emphasis, within overall agreement on basic principle. This is particularly to be expected in the burgeoning American conservative movement of today—and for two reasons. In the first place, the tone of the conservative mind, with its aversion to the narrowly ideological and its respect for the human person, is alien to the concept of a "party line" and so is generous to individual differences of stress on this or that aspect of a general outlook. But more specifically, the principles which inspire the contemporary American conservative movement are developing as the fusion of two different streams of thought. The one, which, for want of a better word, one may call the "traditionalist," puts its primary emphasis upon the authority of transcendent truth and the necessity of a political and social order in accord with the constitution of being. The other, which, again for want of a better word, one may call "libertarian," takes as its first principle in political affairs the freedom of the individual person and emphasizes the restriction of the power of the state and the maintenance of the free-market economy as guarantee of that freedom.

Before the challenge of modern collectivism, hostile alike to transcendent truth and to individual freedom, traditionalist and libertarian have found common cause and tend more and more to work together on the practical political level. But further, the common source in the *ethos* of

Western civilization from which flow both the traditionalist and the libertarian currents, has made possible a continuing discussion which is creating the fusion that is contemporary American conservatism. That fused position recognizes at one and the same time the transcendent goal of human existence and the primacy of the freedom of the person, a value based upon transcendent considerations. And it maintains that the duty of men is to seek virtue; but it insists that men cannot in actuality do so unless they are free from the constraint of the physical coercion of an unlimited state. For the simulacrum of virtuous acts brought about by the coercion of superior power is not virtue, the meaning of which resides in the free choice of good over evil.

Therefore, the conservative—who understands also that power in this world will always exist and cannot be wished out of existence—stands for division of power, in order that those who hold it may balance each other and the concentration of overweening power be foreclosed. He stands for the limitation of the power of the state, division of power within the state, a free economy, and prescriptive protection of the rights of individual persons and groups of individual persons against the state. But he does not see the state as an absolute evil; he regards it as a necessary institution, so long as it is restricted to its natural functions: the preservation of domestic peace and order, the administration of justice, and defense against foreign enemies.

In the political sphere the conservative consensus presently emerging in the United States regards freedom as an end; but, although it is an end at the political level, it is a means—as is the whole political structure—to the higher ends of the human person. Without reference to those ends, it is meaningless. While that conservative consensus regards the untrammeled state as the greatest of political evils, it does not regard the state itself as evil so long as it is limited to its proper functions, so long as the force it wields is effectively limited by a constitutional understanding of the bounds beyond which that force may not intrude upon the sacred sphere of the individual person, and so long as that understanding is enforced by division and balance of powers.

The American conservative today, therefore, although he owes much to the libertarian stream in Western thought—its deep concern with freedom, its analysis of the political structure in terms of freedom, its understanding of the vital importance of the free-market economy for a free modern society—cannot accept the fundamental philosophical position, sometimes rationalist, sometimes utilitarian, which is the historical foundation of pure libertarianism. He cannot posit freedom as an absolute end nor can he, considering the condition of man, deny the role of the state as an institution necessary to protect the freedoms of individual persons from molestation, whether through domestic or foreign force. He is not, in a word, an utopian. He knows that power exists in the world and that it must be controlled, not ignored in wishful utopian thinking.

The contemporary American conservative not only rejects the authoritarian extremes of nineteenth-century conservatism and the extremes of nineteenth-century rationalist and utilitarian liberalism, but, in a sense, he goes behind the so often sterile nineteenth-century conservative-liberal controversy, to found his outlook upon that earlier synthesis of belief in transcendent value and in human freedom which the Founders of the Republic embodied in their lives and actions, discursively expressed in their writings ant their debates, and bequeathed to us in the body politic they constituted.

Their political concern was the establishment of freedom and its preservation, but they understood that freedom is meaningless unless founded upon "the laws of Nature and of Nature's God." The protection of the free energies of free individuals, so that they might in liberty strive to live according to those laws, was their most intimate concern. But they knew that in the defense of liberty a properly constituted state is necessary, not only to "establish Justice [and] insure domestic Tranquillity" but also to "provide for the common defense." They did not content themselves with abstract analyses of liberty; they proclaimed in unambiguous tones, "Give me liberty or give me death." To that wager of fate, "with a firm reliance on the Protection of Divine Providence," they pledged "our Lives, our Fortunes, and our sacred Honor."

"Providence," "honor," "valor," are concepts that the dry utilitarianism of the "pure libertarian" cannot compass. The pity is that when the soul cannot respond to those words, all the brave intellectual structure turns to cobwebs; and the champion of a freedom unfounded on the deep nature of man and the constitution of being pipes out: "Give me liberty if it doesn't mean risking war: give me liberty, but not at the risk of nuclear death."

*Freedom or Virtue?**

L. Brent Bozell

> The..."libertarian" takes as [his] first principle in political
> affairs the freedom of the individual person and empha-
> sizes the restriction of the power of the state and the
> maintenance of the free-market economy as guarantee of
> that freedom.
> ...the "traditionalist" puts [his] primary emphasis upon
> the authority of transcendent truth and the necessity of a
> political and social order in accord with the constitution
> of being.
> —"The Twisted Tree of Liberty" by Frank S. Meyer
> *National Review*, January 16, 1962

Frank Meyer has labored earnestly in recent years to
promote and justify modern American conservatism as a
"fusion" of the libertarian and traditionalist points of view.
His "Twisted Tree," though it read out of the movement
that curious breed of anti-anti-Communist recently
spawned by nihilistic libertarianism, was essentially a re-

---

*This essay appears as it did in the September 1, 1962 issue of
National Review.

statement of the thesis that a symbiosis of the two schools, if the contribution of each is properly understood, is not only possible but necessary. Meyer has been by no means alone in trying to keep order in conservatism's divided house. While he was perhaps the first to identify the contenders generically, and to name the terms for peaceful co-existence, he has been ably seconded by others, notably Stanton Evans, who has made Professor Morton Auerbach's allegations of right-wing schizophrenia ("Do-It-Yourself Conservatism?" *NR*, January 30, 1962) his special concern. Still others, less persuaded than Meyer and Evans of the theoretical cogency of fusionist apologetics, have helped, too—by bearing their misgivings in silence for the sake of conservative unity.

Now I venture no prediction about the political fate of the Meyer-Evans effort—either as to its ability to hold the conservative movement together, or, more to the point, as to whether it will succeed in midwifing the movement to power. After all, the Liberal collapse is creating a power vacuum into which almost anything might move. I do question, however, whether the libertarian-traditionalist amalgam, as the fusionists define it, is *worth* bringing to power. For I doubt whether a movement dominated by libertarianism can be responsive to the root causes of Western disintegration. And we should not make any mistake about this. A movement that can accommodate libertarianism's axiom *is* dominated by it: if freedom is the *"first* principle" in politics, virtue is, at best, the second one; and the programmatic aspects of the movement that affirms that hierarchy will be determined accordingly.

Let us, then, look at the argument by which the fusionists arrive at the primacy of freedom and see whether it is persuasive. If we find the argument wanting, it will then be time to ask whether the theoretical difficulties are worth fretting about.

"The conservative believes," Evans writes, "ours is a God-centered, and therefore an ordered, universe [and] that man's purpose is to shape his life to the patterns of order proceeding from the Divine center of life." Meyer calls this purpose "the transcendent goal of human existence." We may accept these two statements as a fair rendering of the "traditionalist emphasis." Evans adds (and of course Meyer agrees) that man is "hampered" in fulfilling his purpose by "a fallible intellect and vagrant will"—a condition some traditionalists would call original sin.

And now the transition to the "libertarian emphasis." Since he holds these root beliefs, Evans goes on, the *conservative's first concern is that man restrain his appetites by the imperatives of right choice—choice which can take place only in circumstances favoring volition.* This is one of the two reasons, he explains (the other we will consider in due course), why "limitation of government power becomes the highest *political* objective of conservatism." (The emphasis is mine.) Meyer puts the transition this way: the "fused position...maintains that the duty of men is to seek virtue; but it insists that men can not in actuality do so unless they are free from the constraints of the physical coercion of an unlimited state."

The argument is fast, and we will do well to slow it down a bit. Note that there are three propositions implicit in what we have just read: A. Man cannot restrain his "appetites" meaningfully—i.e., pursue virtue—without choosing to do so. B. His ability to choose meaningfully and thus to restrain his appetites depends, to a significant degree, on external "circumstances." C. The *more* these circumstances favor the choice, the *better* he can restrain his appetites and so achieve virtue; and conversely, as these circumstances become unfavorable, the opportunities for virtue diminish accordingly—and theoretically they can shrink, as Evans' word "only" and Meyer's flat "cannot" suggest, all the way to the zero point.

For the moment we may accept proposition A as true: the sense in which choice may *not* be necessary to virtue is not germane at this point. Proposition B, however—that the choice necessary to virtue can be affected by external circumstances—deserves our closest attention. It is key: if it is true, then proposition C, with its corollary that limitation of government power should be considered the highest political good, is probably true also; while if it is not true, this particular argument for libertarianism falls to the ground.

Let us go back to Evans' contention that "man's purpose is to shape his life to the [divine] patterns of order" (or Meyer's variant, "the duty of men is to seek virtue") in order to make sure we understand their meaning. And let us ask them, why is this man's purpose and his duty?

I think there are two possible answers to such a question. One is that God desires—for its own sake—a human order that conforms to the transcendent order, and therefore that He measures virtue by the extent to which human action existentially reflects divine norms. But this answer is certainly not the one Meyer and Evans would give. Under such a view of things, man's concern is simply to establish temporal conditions conducive to God-approved human action, and while leaving matters to individual choice may be useful in some instance, there is no *a priori* need for freedom at all. The other possibility is that God wants man to "prove himself"—or, in Christian terms, to *earn* salvation. This we may assume, until they tell us otherwise, is exactly Meyer's and Evans' meaning. (While there is a formidable taboo against using religious terminology in political discussions, we will do well to disregard it for the moment if we want to grasp the problem, at root a theological one, that fusionists, and I think conservatives in general, are ultimately concerned with.)

Now if earning salvation is what we are talking about, we will have to face up to the problem of whether it is possible for one man to damage another man's chances for it—e.g., by restricting the exercise of his freedom.

Christian teaching is generally to the contrary. How so? It postulates a free will. In doing so, it presupposes a psychological situation in which the intellect entertains conflicting "appetites," or "goods," as alternative courses of action—and turns them over to the will for selection. These alternatives are seldom, if ever, presented for judgment solely on their merits: the choice is invariably "loaded," in the sense that every good carries along with it a certain amount of baggage—the sanctions imposed by habit, education, laws and whatnot—that, in net effect, weights the scales toward one alternative or the other. The mystery of freedom which we feel, or take on faith, but cannot demonstrate is that in spite of these sanctions an element of spontaneity remains. And when this spontaneity (Christian teaching goes on) figures in the selection of the "greater" good over the "lesser" one, as determined by each man's conscience, merit accrues and a step has been taken toward salvation.

But this is simply another way of saying that morally significant choice is a *psychic* event. The good will is the will that adverts to the "better" object as defined by conscience; and it does not cease to be good when it is unable, because of external circumstances, to convert that psychic commitment into *action*. The good will of the man who wants to go to church on Sunday—and would if he could—is not defeated by the "circumstance" that the churches in his country have been shut down. Neither is his virtue diminished, nor his claim to salvation impaired. Moreover—a second dispensation—while the choice spectrum will vary widely from individual to individual both in quality and quantity (variances that can indeed be caused by external circumstances), such disparities are not significant in this context: the fact that the choices open to a Papuan are few and unappetizing to our own palates does not cheat him of reward—or penalty—for such choices as he *is* called upon to make.

What we are saying, then, is that *the freedom that is necessary to virtue is presumably a freedom no man will ever be without.* Morally significant freedom is merely an aspect of the human condition: it is indispensable, but it is also inalienable. The Soviet citizen is every bit as "free" to earn salvation as his American counterpart; he will "prove himself," or fail to, in an area that is beyond the reach of the KGB. And while there is nothing arresting about this presumption—surely it is among the most ordinary of theological commonplaces—it must have tremendous implications for political theory. For if moral freedom is beyond the reach of politics, surely politics has better things to do than making the preservation of moral freedom its chief preoccupation.

But perhaps *we* are moving too fast. Let us try to anticipate the fusionists' reply. They will not, I think, deny that salvation is what they have in mind. But they probably will protest that salvation was not *all* they have in mind. And the protest will very likely develop along these lines:

Granted that man's first purpose is to get to Heaven, and granted, too, that God's justice guarantees every man a fair opportunity to get there: still—God does not want to see a race of stunted men hobbling across the line. After all, man has some value *qua man*. He is brimming with potentialities for living, working, creating—for understanding: God made him that way; surely it is God's will that these potentialities be fulfilled. However—the voice of the Renaissance goes on—in order to explore, to understand, to realize these potentialities man must be free—free to walk the depths of hell or scale the pinnacles of sublimity *on his own two feet*. For society to try to assist man in this adventure, either with its hobbles or with its crutches, is to deny him the opportunity to be a whole man: a man. And by that token he is denied access to true virtue. As Meyer explains: *"the simulacrum of virtuous acts brought about by the coercion of superior power is not virtue, the meaning of which resides in the free choice of good over evil."* (The emphasis is mine.)

Very well. Let us agree for the moment that virtue is not necessarily to be equated with the merit that qualifies for salvation—that there is, in other words, a second order of

virtue, which we may call humanistic virtue since it constitutes the fulfillment of man's human nature. Let us,
however, make sure we understand the rules of the game
of this second realm, as they are understood by Meyer and
others who would have us accept libertarianism's "first
principle." The question of divorce will do as well as any
other for this purpose. Meyer, one gathers from his writings, takes a sacramental view of marriage, and so considers
the preservation of it to be a virtuous act. He is therefore
qualified to help us solve the following problem:

X, an American, has tired of his wife; under the laws of
his state, he has ample grounds for divorce; remarriage
prospects are bright; his friends and professional associates
would be sympathetic with the decision. Yet, after duly
considering such factors, he decides against divorce on the
grounds it is—"wrong."

Y, a Spaniard, has tired of *his* wife; Y is unable to get a
divorce in his own country and to travel to France would
impose a formidable economic burden; remarriage prospects in Spain, in any event, are nil; anyway his religion
forbids it—as does his whole tradition; what is more, he
would face a heavy measure of social ostracism; in short, Y
dismisses the idea without giving it a second thought.
Query: by deciding to preserve his marriage, who—X or
Y—has acted more virtuously? Meyer's answer (and who
would disagree?): X of course. His decision was the tougher
by far; Y's choice was almost reflexive, was not therefore
really "free" at all.

And it follows—does it not?—that if we are seriously
interested in maximizing opportunities for virtue, something will have to be done about Spain. Her laws, traditions,

customs interfere with freedom. They are "crutches"—
kick them away. And in the United States, conditions are
not entirely satisfactory either. We will want to make our
own divorce laws even laxer. We will also want to launch
a public education campaign (privately endowed of course)
aimed at breaking down residual social prejudices; and
perhaps, to help overcome the mechanical difficulties, a
special fund could be set aside for periodic newspaper
notices advising dissatisfied spouses of the most convenient cut-rate agency or mail order house. We will do our
best, in other words, to reduce the "constraints" of "superior power," confident that if Mr. X can stick by his guns
under these conditions, he will really be virtuous. It is not
that we favor divorce, mind you; it is just that we want
virtuous men.

Is the *reductio ad absurdum* unfair? On the contrary: I
submit that the inner logic of the dictum that virtue-not-
freely-chosen is not virtue at all leads inescapably to the
burlesque of reason we have suggested. If freedom is the
"*first* principle" of the search for virtue, if as Meyer writes
at another point, it is "the *precondition* of a good society,"
then, by definition, there is no superior principle that can
be invoked, at any stage, against the effort to maximize
freedom—there is no point at which men are entitled to
stop hauling down the "props" which every rational society
in history has erected to promote a virtuous citizenry.
(True, the libertarian view permits measures for preserving the public order—the argument that no man should
have the liberty to deny another man liberty; our point is
that it permits none for the purpose of encouraging and
aiding virtue.)

The libertarian may object that it is only *state* props that he wants to dismantle—that those created by tradition, custom, religion, in other words, are permissible under certain conditions. But on his own showing he has no business making such a distinction. There are, of course, vital differences between "state" and "social" sanctions, but they have no bearing on the argument in question here—namely, that maximum freedom of choice is essential to individual virtue. For as we have seen earlier, restriction of free choice consists in sanctions of various kinds that accompany alternative courses of action as they are presented to the will. But the relative strength of these sanctions, obviously, is not necessarily a function of their source. Social disapproval can be as persuasive a deterrent against scribbling on walls as the threat of a legal fine; habit and education will often "load" the choice against stealing more effectively than the larceny laws. In short, libertarianism's first command—maximize freedom—applies with equal vigor to all of society's activities; and the meaning of the command, in effect, is this: *virtue must be made as difficult as possible.* While only a few men, if any, can be expected to meet the challenge successfully, the proliferation of unvirtuous acts in the objective order is one of the prices that must be paid for the fulfillment of heroic man....

Now there is nothing to prevent the fusionists from arguing that this command is conducive, as Meyer puts it, to "a political and social order in accord with the constitution of being." But Meyer is not speaking of the constitution of being envisioned by the Christian metaphysic. If there is any metaphysical basis for such a view of life, it is the existentialism of Jean-Paul Sartre—the doctrine that man is all potentiality, i.e., all freedom. In the existentialist view, man has no inherent nature—no essence—and therefore no end other than to work out a nature from his potentialities, each man for himself. In the beginning, this is an optimistic view of life, full of the spirit of individual adventure and creativity, and it ends in despair because the burden of autonomy—since it is not ordained by the true constitution of being—is too heavy.

The Christian metaphysic, by contrast, attributes to man a preformed nature, one that is ultimately defined transcendentally in terms of his origin and destiny. Man's nature, moreover, is totally integrated with that of the rest of being, so that a common effort is envisioned on the part of all creation to conform to what Evans calls the "patterns of order." *Man's* nature is such, however, that he, uniquely among created beings, has the capacity to deviate from the patterns of order—to, as it were, repudiate his nature: i.e., he is free. So viewed, freedom is hardly a blessing; add the ravages of original sin and it is the path to disaster. It follows that if individual man is to have any hope of conforming with his nature, he needs all of the help he can get. That is why the role of grace is so vital to the Christian view of things, not only supernatural grace, but the natural grace that springs forth from man's constructs: his institutions, his customs, his laws—the ones that have been inspired by his better angel and that remain in time to give nourishment to all the human race. And that, in turn, is why the Christian view, which begins in despair, ends in optimism.

"Go...and teach all nations." These are the marching

orders of Christianity, and, from a theological viewpoint, its central operational command. God's purpose, if we may put it so, is twofold: to give the widest possible access to supernatural grace—that is, to magnify the Christian Church; and to establish temporal conditions conducive to human virtue—that is, to build a Christian *civilization*. The latter purpose is the genesis and justification for the notion that Western civilization, being the historical fruit of the Incarnation—and so, in a manner of speaking, "God's civilization"—must be preserved at all costs, and itself magnified. There is not a drop of chauvinism in the idea, for it has to do entirely—as the classicists taught—with the relationship between the good commonwealth and the virtuous man. When a commonwealth builds according to the divine patterns of order, then it is in a position to help man conform to his nature, which is the meaning of virtue. The institutions the commonwealth promotes are the important thing—its family arrangements, its schools, its churches, the kind of government it has; for all of these combine to generate what Willmore Kendall calls its public orthodoxy. Now to the extent a public orthodoxy tends to reflect the divine patterns of order, it also tends to encourage a virtuous citizenry. Of course such external inducements to virtue can never be entirely, or even very, successful: to suppose that through man's artifacts the human race, or any member of it, can be perfected in history is to partake of the modern gnosticism upon which both Liberalism and Communism are grounded. But such inducements can ease the way to virtue. That is the reason for the marching orders.

Which invites reconsideration of an earlier question: Is

freedom an *a priori* requirement for virtue? We can agree that the freer the choice—i.e., the more difficult it is—the greater the *merit*. But if, by definition, the virtuous act is one that conforms with man's nature, with the divine patterns of order—is the kind of heroic freedom envisioned by libertarian doctrine essential to such an act? Every day on his way to work A slips a dime to the blind lady at the street corner; it is pure habit with him. B supports his family as a matter of course; the thought of abandoning it to seek his own pleasure never crosses his mind. C buys a "worthwhile" novel at his book store, though—let us postulate such a weakness—if a well-advertised volume of pornography had not been banned by the state, he would have picked it up instead. Now these acts are, in turn—a) reflexive, b) instinctive, c) coerced by state power. Yet each of them, in itself, is a *virtuous* act if man's virtue consists in conducting himself in conformity with his nature, with the divine patterns of order.

We may go further, since man will always have sufficient moral freedom, i.e., sufficient occasions for "proving himself"—and even for doing so heroically; and since these occasions are basically traceable to his corruption, the ideal to which man should aspire is to *minimize* such occasions—to develop the kind of character that will generate virtuous acts as a matter of course. For as the mystics tell us, true sanctity is achieved only when man loses his freedom—when he is freed of the temptation to displease God.

We may now turn to the second reason, on the fusionists' showing, why limitation of government power would be

our "highest political objective." And we may agree that it
is a "second" argument inasmuch as it proceeds from
fundamentally different premises from those that posit
political freedom as an absolute requirement for personal
virtue. By the same token, however, it does not warrant the
absolutist conclusions libertarians claim for it.

Mr. Evans put the argument thus: "...the reign of appetite is most destructive, and the incentives and opportunities for its exercise most plentiful, when fallible man is
endowed with unlimited power over his fellow beings. If a
man is corrupted in mind and impulse, he is hardly to be
trusted with the unbridled potencies of the state." Evans
adds that the American Constitution reflects this view
inasmuch as it is "premised upon a deep distrust of human
nature and [is] designed to curb its excesses."

Now if we may read "the reign of appetite" to mean the
ascendancy of non-virtue in the objective order (as opposed to the "reign" of personal sinfulness), then the
argument that unlimited state power is conducive to that
ascendancy is, other things being equal, unexceptionable.
For now the argument is focused on *the effects unlimited
power is likely to have on those who exercise it, and derivatively
on the damage they are likely to do the commonwealth they
govern.* And we are looking at nothing more than a restatement of Lord Acton's adage that "power tends to corrupt;
absolute power corrupts absolutely." But note that Acton
did not try to convert this essentially *prudential* judgment
about the dangers of government power into an absolute
rule for restricting government power. He did not, that is
to say—and neither should we—commit the elementary
logical fallacy of turning the proposition, "the state that

governs most will govern worst," into the proposition, "the state that governs least will govern best."

If the judgment is a prudential one, the question in every case will be: *Will this grant of this power, in this instance, for this object, produce a net good for the individual members of the commonwealth?* Such a question will take into account the objections libertarians regularly, and usually wisely, interpose to accretions of state power: government will do the job badly; one aggrandizement will lead to another; a concession today will make it harder to stand firm tomorrow; and so on. And a thousand times more often than not—given the kind of claims government makes these days—the prudent decision will be against the grant of power and in favor of leaving the individual and private groups on their own. But not always. The good commonwealth, taking the measure of its governors, and the prospects for their corruption, may charge them with, say, building roads, or maintaining a postal system, or passing anti-obscenity laws, or giving tax-exemption to its churches.

This is not to say (for I would hope not to be understood as endorsing theocracy) that the good commonwealth will charge the state with *discovering* and *defining* the elements of virtue. Rather, it will look upon the state merely as one potential instrument among many others for articulating and thus defending the community consensus about such things; and while prudence will dictate severe limitations even on this role, prudence does not go so far, I am saying, as to forbid acknowledgment of God's existence in the state's schools.

Once we have decided to view the dangers of state power as but one element among others—a very important one,

to be sure—in a prudential judgment about the requirements of the good commonwealth, we have made considerable headway in our thinking about how to build such a
commonwealth. We have, that is to say, liberated the
discussion from the ideological straitjacket in which libertarian dogma confines it—the dogma about the "natural
functions" of the state. These are, as Meyer never tires of
telling us, [1] *the preservation of domestic peace and order,*
[2] *the administration of justice, and* [3] *defense against
foreign enemies.* Any activities beyond these three, according to the argument, are by definition—and so without
further discussion—evil.

I do not think Meyer or the other fusionists will ever be
able to explain to the uninitiated the mystery of the trinitarian
state—except, possibly, in terms of the argument for heroic freedom we have already considered. They will certainly not be able to explain on the strength of an organic
view of man and society why, e.g., it is "natural" for the
state to lock up a thief, and "unnatural" for the state to
launch a program against juvenile delinquency. Nor—
assuming that what actually happens in the real world has
some bearing on what is "natural"—can they realistically
hypothesize future conditions under which the trinitarian
concept will be adopted; nor point to any past moment in
history when men have actually organized a society in this
way; nor cite any serious thinker in back of the nineteenth
century who has suggested men try to do so. In short, the
dogma of ritualistic libertarianism is hardly less far from
reality than that of ritualistic Liberalism, and it presents the
same kind of barriers to acquiring wisdom about the good
commonwealth.

This is perhaps the place to nail the notion, so often advanced by the fusionists, that the American Constitution is an expression of the libertarian-traditionalist compromise—i.e., that in the name of accommodating human nature, the Constitution underwrites the archly limited state. On the face of it, it is the purest fancy to suggest that American constitutional theory has anything in common with the libertarian teaching about the threefold function of the *genus* state. The individual American States, let us remember, marched into the Constitutional Convention with *full sovereign powers*—the three Meyer mentions plus several dozen others he does not; and the problem to which the convention delegates so brilliantly addressed themselves was how to organize and distribute those powers so as to promote their most beneficial exercise. The framers' governing principle was, of course, the one often attributed to Madison: that concentration of power leads to its abuse. And the remedy they invoked was also Madison's: the way to block the pernicious ambitions of "factions," Madison argued, is to distribute power as widely as possible within clearly defined boundaries. (While it is true that subsequent judicial construction of the Constitution, making the Bill of Rights applicable to the States, seems to place some powers altogether out of bounds—even these proscriptions are not absolute, as a glance at the Constitution's amending clause will quickly verify.)

Under the American system of government, in other words, the genus state—with its municipal, state, and national offices, and its popular residuary—potentially has plenary powers. Felicitously, under the original concept, these powers were distributed in a fashion that closely approximates the principle of subsidiarity—the idea that the quest for the common good begins with the individual man and will ascend to increasingly collectivized levels only under necessity, and always with a prudential concern for the dangers of going higher. In short, much freedom was envisioned by the founders of such a system because freedom is highly useful in achieving the good commonwealth. But there is not a hint of the ideology of freedom in what they produced—not a word suggesting that freedom is *the goal* of the commonwealth.

It is a mistake to make demi-gods out of the framers, or to read as a piece of scripture what they wrote. But, as perhaps the only group of men in modern history to have set their minds to the task of constructing a commonwealth on the basis of prudence, and therefore free from ideology, they deserve considerable reverence, and are a fit object for imitation.

Uneasy Cousins

ROBERT NISBET

By common assent modern conservatism, as political philosophy, springs from Edmund Burke, chiefly from his *Reflections on the Revolution in France*, published in 1790. A brilliantly prescient analysis of the Revolution and its new and fateful modes of power over individual lives, the *Reflections* is also, through its running asides and *obiter dicta*, one of the most profound treatments of the nature of political legitimacy ever written. Modern political conservatism, as we find it in a European philosophical tradition from about 1800 on, originates in Burke's insistence upon the rights of society and its historically formed groups (such as family, neighborhood, guild, and church) against the "arbitrary power" of a political government. Individual liberty, Burke argued—and it remains the conservative thesis to this day—is only possible within the context of a plurality of social authorities, moral codes, and historical traditions, all of which, in organic articulation, serve at one and the same time as "the inns and resting places" of the human spirit and intermediary barriers to the power of the state over the individual. The influence of Burke's *Reflections* was immediate, and all the major works of European philosophical conservatism—those of Bonald, de Maistre, the young Lamennais, Hegel, Haller, Donoso y Cortes, Southey and Coleridge, among others—in the early nineteenth century are rooted, as their authors without exception acknowledged, in Burke's seminal volume.

Burke, it should be stressed, had a political-ideological record leading up to his famous *Reflections* that was not regarded in his time, and would not be ordinarily thought of today, as quintessentially conservative. From boyhood he had been an ardent admirer of the Glorious Revolution of 1688, an event which had taken place four decades before his birth. When troubles with the American colonies broke out in the 1760s, Burke threw himself without reserve on the side of the colonists, and his parliamentary speeches on the Americans and on what he regarded as the hateful practices of the British government are of course classics. He may not have endorsed the colonies' decision to go to war, and to seek a complete break with England, but his sympathies lay nonetheless with those Englishmen who had created the New World of America. It is worth recalling that, as with respect to the Americans, some of Burke's most powerful speeches in Parliament were delivered in behalf of India and its traditional culture and in fierce opposition to Warren Hastings (whom Burke sought unsuccessfully to indict) and the British East India company for its depredations in India. And for all his love of England and English ways, Burke was unrelenting in his criticism of the government for its treatment of Ireland, his own birthplace. In sum, it was with good reason that Burke's close friend, that essential Tory, Dr. Johnson, could worry over Burke's whiggism.

Turning now to the foundations of contemporary libertarianism, of classical liberalism, we can go back to John Locke's *Second Treatise*, to the writings of Montesquieu in France, those of Jefferson in America, and Adam Smith in England. But the securest and most vivid source of libertarianism lies in J.S. Mill's *On Liberty*, published in 1859, the same year in which Darwin's *Origin of Species* appeared (which has its own relation to classical libertarianism, through its central thesis of what the classical liberals called the free market).

In *On Liberty* Mill expresses at the beginning his famous "one very simple principle." Mill writes: "The sole end for which mankind are warranted, individually and collectively, in interfering with the liberty of action of any of their number is self-protection.... His own good, either physical or moral, is not a sufficient warrant." I suggest that Mill's "one very simple principle" is the core of contemporary libertarianism. It is necessary, though, to note Mill's immediate qualifications to the principle, qualifications which may or may not be acceptable to the majority of libertarians in our own day. Thus we learn that the principle does not apply to those below their legal majority, an abridgment that large numbers of high school and college students today would ridicule and reject. Nor does the principle hold for those Mill rather cryptically identifies as being "in a state to require being taken care of by others," a state that must include all those on welfare in our society as well as those whom Mill probably had chiefly in mind, the chronically ill and the mentally deficient. Mill categorically excludes from this principle of liberty all peoples on earth who are in "backward states of society." For them, he declares, despotism remains necessary, albeit as enlightened as possible, until through social evolution these peoples reach the level of modern Western civilization.

Later in the essay Mill goes so far as to deny the principle of liberty to those around us who are, in his words, "nuisances" to others. And, he continues, "no one pretends that actions should be as free as opinions." In its bald statement Mill's one very simple principle would most certainly give legitimacy to contemporary pornography in all spheres as well as to noisy, order-disrupting, potentially violent street demonstrations. But with the qualifications just cited, it is far from evident that Mill's view of legitimate freedom would give sanction to contemporary license—moral, political, or religious. It is impossible not to believe that even in bald, abstract statement, Mill's single simple principle was intended to apply only to people formed intellectually and morally as Mill himself was. But such observations do not affect the sheer power that has been exerted especially during the past half-century, by Mill's principle—in philosophy, the social sciences, theology, law, and most recently in popular morality. (Looking at the scene around us, who can seriously doubt that the counter-culture won the important battles in its war against traditional American morality, commencing in the 1950s and reaching its high point in the late 1960s? In essence these battles were waged in the spirit of Mill's one very simple principle. Mill may have taken seriously the checks and limits he prescribed, but others, looking at the principle in the discrete, abstract, and categorically imperative form in which Mill set it down, have felt no similar obligation.)

So much for the roots of conservatism and libertarianism. Now I shall turn to the more important growths from these roots which lie around us today. What are they, their likenesses and differences, assessed by the criteria of the conservative and the libertarian mind respectively? For the sake of clarity I shall begin with what the two minds appear to have in common.

First is common dislike of the intervention of government, especially national, centralized government, in the economic, social, political, and intellectual lives of citizens. Edmund Burke was quite as adamant in this regard (see his strictures on French centralization and nationalization in the *Reflections*) as Mill or any other classical liberal, and that position has been maintained to the present. Doubtless conservatives are more willing than libertarians to see the occasional necessity of suspension or abrogation of this position toward national government, as with respect to national defense. In general, however, over a substantial period of time, conservatism may be seen quite as clearly as libertarianism to be a philosophy anchored in opposition to statism. Certainly by comparison with what today passes for liberalism, progressivism, populism, and social democracy or socialism, there is very little difference to be found between libertarians and conservatives regarding attitudes toward the political state.

Second, and again by comparison with the other groups I have just cited, there is a great deal of consensus among

conservatives and libertarians as to what legitimate equality in society should consist of. Such equality is, in a word,
legal. Again we may refer to Burke and Mill on this matter.
For both, equality before the law was vital to the flourishing
of individual freedom. Nothing in the contemporary writings of libertarians and conservatives seems to suggest that
anything more than an occasional nuance or emphasis
separates the two groups when it comes to equality. There
is equal condemnation of what has come to be called
equality of result, of social condition, or of income or
wealth.

Third, there is a common belief in the necessity of
freedom, most notably *economic* freedom. Again, there
appear to be more conservatives than libertarians who on
occasion are prepared to endorse occasional infringement
upon individual freedom through laws and regulatory
agencies designed to protect or lift up one or other disadvantaged group. One thinks of British Toryism in the
nineteenth century or of Senator Robert Taft on public
housing in the late 1940s. Inasmuch as few if any all-out
libertarians have yet faced the kinds of pressure in high
public office which come from groups demanding one or
other entitlement or exemption, it is not possible to com-
pare libertarians and conservatives in terms of demonstrated adherence to philosophical principles when political practicalities and long-range ends are involved.

Fourth, there is a common dislike of war and, more
especially, of the war-society this country knew in 1917
and 1918 under Woodrow Wilson and again under FDR in
World War II. Libertarians may protest this, and with some
ground. The complete libertarian is certainly more likely to

resist in overt fashion than is the conservative, for whom respect for nation and for patriotism is likely to be decisive even when it is a war he opposes. Even so, I think there is enough common ground, at least with respect to principle, to put conservatives and libertarians together. Let us remember that beginning with the Spanish-American War, which the conservative McKinley opposed strongly, and coming down through each of the wars this century in which the United States became involved, the principal opposition to American entry came from those elements of the economy and social order which were generally identifiable as conservative—whether "middle western isolationist," traditional Republican, central European ethnic, small business, or however we wish to designate such opposition. I am certainly not unmindful of the libertarian opposition to war that could come from a Max Eastman and a Eugene Debs and from generally libertarian conscientious objectors in considerable numbers in both world wars, but the solid and really formidable opposition to American entry came from those closely linked to business, church, local community, family, and traditional morality. (Tocqueville correctly identified this class in America as reluctant to engage in any foreign war because of its predictable impact chiefly upon business and commerce and upon other social and moral activities as well.) *This* was the element in American life, not the minuscule libertarian element, that both Woodrow Wilson and FDR had to woo, persuade, propagandize, convert, and, in some instances virtually terrorize, in order to pave the way for eventual entry by U.S. military forces in Europe and Asia.

As some of the foregoing has already suggested, there is

shared dislike by libertarians and conservatives of what today passes for liberalism: the kind that is so widely evident in the schools, the established churches, the universities, and, above all, the media. In passing, I would like to suggest that conservatism, on the historical record, has done more to oppose, circumvent, or defeat specific manifestations of this so-called liberalism than has libertarianism. I can recall many a conservative in the 1930s speaking out against Social Security, the AAA, the NRA, and the free-wheeling, increasingly arrogant National Education Association with its canonization of progressive libertarianism for tots in kindergarten. Perhaps there were some libertarians then also active, but I don't recall. However, I'm not cavilling. History decides these things. There were far more identified, politically active conservatives than libertarians in the America of that day. In the next decade or two, things may well become reversed.

Now to differences, or some of them, at any rate. Everything at the moment suggests that the *differences* between conservatism, all-out or neo-, and libertarianism, anarcho- or constitutional, will loom increasingly large and divisive. By and by, it will be impossible for the phrases "libertarian-conservative" and "conservative-libertarian" to be other than oxymoronic: like referring to a mournful optimist or a cruel kindness. Here too I shall avoid cases and cling to principles and perspectives.

First is the contrasting way in which the two groups perceive the population. Conservatives, from Burke on, have tended to see the population in the manner medieval

legists and philosophical realists (in contrast to nominal-
ists) saw it: as composed, not of individuals directly, but of
the natural groups within which individuals invariably
live—family, locality, church, region, social class, nation,
and so on. Individuals exist, of course, but they cannot be
seen or comprehended save in terms of social identities
which are inseparable from groups and associations. If
modern conservatism came into existence essentially
through such a work as Burke's attack on the French
Revolution, it is because the Revolution, so often in the
name of the individual and his natural rights, destroyed or
diminished the traditional groups—guild, aristocracy, pa-
triarchal family, church, school, province, etc.—which
Burke declared to be the irreducible and constitutive
molecules of society. Such early conservatives as Burke,
Bonald, Haller, and Hegel (of *The Philosophy of Right*), and
such conservative liberals as the mature Lamennais and of
course Tocqueville, saw individualism—that is, the absolute doctrine of individualism—as being as much of a
menace to social order and true freedom as the absolute
doctrine of nationalism. Indeed, they argued, it is the
pulverizing of society into a sandheap of individual par-
ticles, each claiming natural rights, that makes the arrival
of collectivist nationalism inevitable.

Libertarians are not blind to the existence of groups and
associations, nor to the traditions and customs which are
their cement, and it would be absurd to characterize
libertarians as undiscriminating enemies of all forms of
association. They do not propose a return to the
Enlightenment's vaunted state of nature. Only rarely does
a libertarian sound like a clone of Max Stirner. They are as

devoted to the principle of voluntary association as any conservative. And we should not forget that the libertarian anarchism of a Proudhon or Kropotkin was based upon a social order of groups, not abstract, Godwinian individuals. Even so, reading the libertarian journals and reviews of the last several years, I am convinced that there is a much larger egoist-hormone in the libertarian physiology than in the conservative. More and more, one has the impression that for libertarians today, as for natural law theorists in the seventeenth century, individuals are alone real; institutions are but their shadows. I believe a state of mind is developing among libertarians in which the coercions of family, church, local community, and school will seem almost as inimical to freedom as those of the political government. If so, this will most certainly widen the gulf between libertarians and conservatives.

Which leads to a second major difference between the two groups. The conservative philosophy of liberty proceeds from the conservative philosophy of *authority*. The existence of authority in the *social* order staves off encroachments of power from the political sphere. Conservatism, from Burke on, has perceived society as a plurality of authorities. There is the authority of the parent over the small child, of the priest over the communicant, the teacher over the pupil, the master over the apprentice, and so on. Society as we actually observe it is a network or tissue of such authorities; they are really numberless when we think of the kinds of authority which lie within even the smallest of human groups and relationships. Such authority may be loose, gentle, protective, and designed to produce individuality, but it is authority nevertheless. For the conservative, individual freedom lies in the interstices of social and moral authority. Only because of the restraining and guiding effects of such authority does it become possible for human beings to sustain so liberal a political government as that which the Founding Fathers designed in this country and which flourished in England from the late seventeenth century on. Remove the social bonds, as the more zealous and uncompromising of libertarian individualists have proposed ever since William Godwin, and you emerge with, not a free but a chaotic people, not creative but impotent individuals. Human nature, Balzac correctly wrote, cannot endure a moral vacuum.

To argue, as some libertarians have, that a solid, strong body of authority in society is incompatible with individual creativity is to ignore or misread cultural history. Think of the great cultural efflorescences of the fifth century B.C. in Athens, of first century Augustan Rome, of the thirteenth century in Europe, of the Age of Louis XIV, and Elizabethan England. One and all, these were ages of social and moral order, powerfully supported by moral codes and political statutes. But the Aeschyluses, Senecas, Roger Bacons, Molières, and Shakespeares flourished nonetheless. Far from feeling oppressed by the hierarchical authority all around him, Shakespeare—about whose copious individuality there surely cannot be the slightest question—is the author of the memorable passage that begins with "Take but degree away, untune that string,/ And hark! what discord follows; each thing meets/ In mere oppugnancy." As A.L. Rowse has documented in detail, the social structure of Shakespeare's England was not only solid, its authority ever evident, but nothing threw such fear into the people as the thought that authority—especially that designed to repulse foreign enemies and to ferret out traitors—might be made too loose and tenuous. Of course such authority could become too insistent at times, and ingenious ways were found by the dramatists and essayists to outwit the government and its censors. After all, it was strong social and moral authority the creative minds were living under—not the oppressive, political-bureaucratic, limitless, invasive, totalitarian governments of the twentieth century.

Finally, it might be noted that the greatest literary presences to appear thus far in the twentieth-century Western culture have nearly all been votaries of tradition and cultural authority. Eliot, Pound, Joyce, Yeats, and others all gave testimony to authority in poem, essay and novel, and all, without exception, saw the eventual death of Western culture proceeding from annihilation of this authority in the names of individualism and of freedom.

To be sure there is—and this is recognized fully by the conservative—a degree of liberty below which nothing of creative significance can be accomplished. Without at least that degree of freedom, no Shakespeare, no Marlowe, no Newton. But what is less often realized, conservatives would say, is that there is a degree of freedom *above which* nothing of creative significance can be, or is likely to be, accomplished. Writers in the late twentieth century do their work in the freest air writers have ever breathed. But it is apparent from the wretched mess of narcissism, self-abuse, self-titillation, and juvenile, regressive craving for the scatological and obscene that the atmosphere has become so rarefied as to have lost its oxygen.

On balance, I would hazard the guess that for libertarians individual freedom, in almost every conceivable domain, is the *highest of all social values*—irrespective of what
forms and levels of moral, aesthetic, and spiritual debase-
ment may prove to be the unintended consequences of
such freedom. For the conservative, on the other hand,
freedom, while important, is but *one of several necessary
values* in the good or just society, and not only may but
should be restricted when such freedom shows signs of
weakening or endangering national security, of doing
violence to the moral order and the social fabric. The
enemy common to libertarians and to conservatives is
what Burke called arbitrary power, but from the conservative viewpoint this kind of power becomes almost inevitable when a population comes to resemble that of Rome
during the decades leading up to the accession of Augustus
in 31 B.C.; of London in the period prior to Puritan and
then Cromwellian rule; of Paris prior to the accession of
Napoleon as ruler of France; of Berlin during most of
Weimar. It is not liberty but chaos and license which,
conservatives would and do say, come to dominate when
moral and social authorities—those of family, neighborhood, local community, job, and religion—have lost their
appeal to human beings. Is it likely that the present age,
that of, say, the last fifty years and, so far as we can now see,
the next couple of decades at very minimum, will ever be
pronounced by later historians as a major age of culture?
Hardly. And can it seriously be thought in this age of *The
Naked Lunch, Oh! Calcutta, The Hustler,* and *Broadway Sex
Live and Explicit* that our decadent mediocrity as a culture
will ever be accounted for in terms of excessive social and

moral authority?

Libertarians, on the other hand, appear to see social and moral authority and despotic political power as elements of a single spectrum, as an unbroken continuity. If, their argument goes, we are to be spared Leviathan we must challenge any and all forms of authority, including those which are inseparable from the social bond. Libertarians seem to me to give less and less recognition to the very substantial difference between the coercions of, say, family, school, and local community and those of the centralized bureaucratic state. For me it is a generalization proved countless times in history that the onset of ever more extreme political-military power has for its necessary prelude the erosion and collapse of the authorities within the social bond which serve to give the individual a sense of identity and security, whose very diversity and lack of *unconditional* power prevent any escape-proof monopoly, and which in the aggregate are the indispensable bulwarks against the invasion of centralized political power—which of course is unconditional. But I do not often find among libertarians these days any clear recognition of the point I have just made.

There is a final area in which the difference between conservatives and libertarians is likely to grow steadily: the nation. I stand by everything I have said in support of social authority, diversity, and pluralism, and in opposition to concentration of national power. I do not have to be instructed on the number of times war and mobilization for and prosecution of war have led to "temporary" centralization and nationalizations which, alas, proved to be permanent. War is, above any other force in history, the basis of centralization and collectivization of the social and economic orders. No conservative can relish, much less seek, war and its attendant militarization of social and civil spheres of society.

Unfortunately we do not live in a clement world so far as conservative and libertarian ideals are concerned. It is a world in which despotisms as huge and powerful as China and (until recently) the Soviet Union survive and prosper—at least in political and diplomatic respects. For the United States to ignore or to profess indifference to the aggressive acts of these and many other military despotisms would be in time suicidal. As Montesquieu wrote in a different context: it takes a power to check a power. Nothing short of a strong, well armed, alert and active American nation can possibly check the Chinese or Cuban nation.

No conservative to my knowledge has ever renounced or reviled the nation, conceived as a cultural and spiritual, as well as political entity. Burke adored the nation. He merely insisted upon seeing it—in vivid contrast to the Jacobins of his day—as a community of communities, as one built upon a diversity of what he called "the smaller patriotisms" such as family and neighborhood. So have conservatives, or the great majority of them, ever since chosen to see the nation. But what conservatives also see in our tie, and with a sharpness of perception lacking among libertarians, is the tenuous condition of the American nation—and of the English and French as well. There is good nationalism and bad. But even good nationalism has become an object of either nostalgia or revulsion in our time. Patriotism, the cement of the nation, has come to be an almost shameful thing. The weakness of American government right now in the world of nations, a weakness that increasingly draws contempt and distrust from nations we desire close cooperation with, and the dearth of leadership in America in whatever sphere, are rooted in a nation that shows increasing signs of moribundity.

Libertarians, whom I herewith stipulate to be as patriotic and loyally American as conservatives, do not, in my judgment, see the national and world picture as I have just drawn it. For them the essential picture is not that of a weakened, softened, and endangered nation in a threatening world, but, rather, an American nation swollen from the juices of nationalism, interventionism, and militarism that really has little to fear from abroad. Conservatives remain by and large devoted to the smaller patriotisms of family, church, locality, job and voluntary association, but they tend to see these as perishable, as destined to destruction, unless the nation in which they exist owns the eminence and international authority it enjoyed in the 1950s. To libertarians, on the other hand, judging from many of their writings and speeches, it is as though the steps necessary to recovery of this eminence and international authority are more dangerous to Americans and their liberties than any aggressive, imperialist totalitarianisms in the world.

Conservatives will, or certainly should, also be alert to these dangers and seek with every possible strength to reduce them. But for conservatives the supreme danger will be, I imagine, and personally hope, the danger posed by current American weakness in a world of dangerously aggressive military despotisms. Nothing at the moment suggests that this consideration will be overriding for libertarians. And it is on this rock above all others that conservatives and libertarians will surely break off altogether what has been from the start an uneasy relationship.

The Need for
Public Authority

WALTER BERNS

Almost thirty years ago, I resigned from Cornell University; at that time the university had just been taken over by students carrying guns, and first the administration and then the faculty collapsed into separate but equally ignominious heaps. My resignation then gained me some fleeting fame, which, I suspect, led to an invitation to address the Philadelphia Society. At this national meeting of 1969 a speaker expressed his concern that certain elements of civility seemed to be disappearing from American society, and he called for government action designed to restore them, or strengthen them. For example, if I remember correctly, he favored such programs as school prayers, and public aid to religious education, and the enforcement of the laws against obscenity. Another speaker gave a paper that might have been entitled, but was not, "the withering away of the state." Its thesis, I recall, was that government was unnecessary, except to provide a defense against international marauders; he promised to return the next year with a paper demonstrating that this defense role, too, could be better performed by private police forces, or armies. Whether he came back to deliver that paper, I do not know.

What struck me at the time was that—assuming these two speakers were both members in good standing—the Philadelphia Society must be, at least potentially, a house divided against itself. What, besides a common dislike of liberals, or of the Democratic party, did its members hold in common? There seemed to be a danger that if the liberals ever folded their tents (or were forced to do so) and filed silently into the night of our history, the Philadelphia Society might face what the liberals themselves would call an identity crisis. It is a fact, I think, that the liberals have been forced in recent years to strike a good many of the tents they have erected over the face of our political landscape, so that the time is at hand when their opponents will have to decide what it is that they are. If my late colleague Robert Nisbet was correct, the choice lies between libertarianism and conservatism. These positions are most probably not, finally, reconcilable, Frank Meyer's work in "fusionism" notwithstanding.

As I shall argue, libertarianism is an extension of the original liberalism, insofar as it depends on the principle of self-interest. Conservatism, on the other hand, is a vestige of the original opposition to the original liberalism, insofar as it depends on the principle of the fatherhood of God and the brotherhood of mankind.

As an outsider, it would be improper of me to attempt to influence the choice of the Philadelphia Society between these two positions, or principles; but, since my topic is "the need for public authority," it would be difficult to avoid saying something relevant to the choice. Besides, some of the members are familiar with my work and, therefore, are sure to know where, on the whole, I stand. In fact, of course, and in this respect my position may be similar to that held by many of the members, a part of me stands in each camp. While living in Washington, I have been given reason to be appalled—appalled all over again— by the size of the federal government and by its attitude toward the rest of the country. For example, I am appalled by a government that sets aside some 50,000 parking places for its employees, the vast majority of them at no charge and the rest at a very nominal charge, and then, in the name of energy conservation, dares to tell the rest of the country to drive no faster than 55 miles per hour. (These parking places in the District of Columbia, incidentally, guarantee that traffic will not move when the snow falls or a farmer's tractor is parked on the 14th Street bridge over the Potomac.) I am appalled when the people who live there and who already enjoy a per capita income some 26 percent higher than the national average dare to argue that the principle of no taxation without representation entitles them to full representation in the Congress. No, living in Washington serves to reinforce an opinion of long standing—an opinion held since I ceased to be a member of the Socialist Party—that the libertarians are at least partly right: we would be better off if a large part of this federal "state" would wither away.

And I suppose that we could all agree, on the whole, where to begin our dismantling of this government: the Department of Energy, for one, then the Federal Trade

Commission, the Department of Education, the Occupational Safety and Health Administration, and so on. We think the economy would be healthier if the government would cease much of its regulation; we might also agree, on the whole again, that we would be better off if the government were to get out of our lives. We might agree with this statement made in a dissenting opinion in a case decided some twelve years ago by the Supreme Court: "The intrusion of government into this domain is symptomatic of the disease of this society. As the years pass the power of the government becomes more and more pervasive. It is a power to suffocate both people and causes" (*Branzburg* vs. *Hayes*, 408 U.S. 665, 724 [1972]). I do not, however, think that all of us would agree with the position taken in that case by that judge, and I doubt that any of us would regard that judge, William O. Douglas, as a hero. He was complaining about the refusal of the majority of the Court to grant newsmen a privilege of not answering questions put to them in a court of law or by a grand jury. Most of us would, I think, say that if President Nixon was required to answer questions put to him by Judge Sirica, then *New York Times* reporters would be required to answer questions put to them by other judges. We do not object to this form of governmental power. Certainly I do not object.

But I am not a libertarian. While I happily support the application of the libertarian principle of self-interest to economic activities—because I think that Adam Smith was right, and because it seems clear to me that capitalism is the only economic system ever devised by the wit of man that puts men to work and guarantees that men will in fact *work*—I cannot support the extension of that principle into other areas. I can state my reason simply: I do not share what appears to be the libertarians' view of the nature of man. This means that I must disagree with Professor Hayek, for instance, when he says it is "conceivable that the spontaneous order which we call society may exist without government." I do not believe it. I do not believe that without government there can be any order, and certainly not a decent order, one in which he and I would care to live. I do not believe it because, like Thomas Hobbes, I think that life in a society that is not governed, that lacks the authority and power of a government, will be "solitary, poor, nasty, brutish and short."

Hobbes might be called the first libertarian; he was the founder of the modern liberal state insofar as he was the first thinker to elaborate the principles of that state. I mean by this that he was the first political philosopher to argue openly that government may be founded on an anti-religious basis, and the first to build a politics that takes its bearings from the natural rights of man, and specifically the right of each man to preserve himself and to do whatever is necessary to preserve himself. This included the right to kill anyone who threatens him. If libertarianism can be defined as the body of thought that opposed government in the name of liberty, or the private life and the private realm, then Hobbes was a libertarian, because he was the first political philosopher to deny altogether the *natural* existence of the public realm. Naturally, i.e., by nature, there is no such things as *a* public, or *the* public. Naturally, there is only a private life.

Those of us who appreciate privacy should not lose sight of our indebtedness to Hobbes. Before him, and for a time after him, it was understood that every human activity was subject to public scrutiny and public control, if not by the state, then by the church, and usually by the state as church. The highest claim to privacy was traditionally made by the philosophers; they claimed that whatever might be said about other activities, at least philosophy ought to be outside the range of public control. But, as I once wrote, we know from Plato's *Republic* that even the philosopher can, in principle, "be made to forgo his privacy...in the best of all possible cities where he will rule as king." In fact, of course, the life of Socrates and the work of Plato can best be understood as an attempt to preserve the philosophic life from public attention and interference. But that only serves to indicate how difficult it is to make the case for privacy, and how much our privacy owes to Hobbes. He was the first philosopher, or to be more precise, the first *political* philosopher, to argue that by nature all was private; that the public realm was artificial in the strict sense of having to be made by man. The success of his enterprise was astonishing. True, the British and Canadians continue to carry coins in their pickets bearing the words *Dei Gratia Regina*—Queen by the Grace of God—but that is merely a vestige of a pre-Hobbesian politics and of little practical consequence. We Americans insist that legitimate government can only come from the will of the people: "To secure these rights," we say, "governments are instituted among men, deriving their just powers from the consent of the governed." According to Thomas Jefferson as well as Thomas Hobbes, no one has by nature and no one has by the grace of God a right to rule another man.

But there is a difference of some magnitude between Hobbes and the libertarians; Hobbes knew that the nature of man required government. That is why he called for a sovereign with absolute powers, the sovereign he denominated Leviathan, the king over all the children of pride.

To repeat: Hobbes taught that by nature man is a private animal, not a public or political animal; that he thinks first of himself, and of others only as objects to be conquered or to be put to his own use. This is why life in the state of nature is a war of everyman against everyman, a war, he says, that ceaseth only in death. This warring can be avoided only by each man yielding his natural rights to the artificial ruler brought into being by the contract that all the "real" men make with each other. This artificial ruler, this Leviathan, is, in principle, an absolute ruler.

In practice, however, this Leviathan will confine himself to keeping the peace and otherwise will leave men alone to pursue their private lives and their private activities, especially their private economic activities. After all, we call the state based on Hobbesian principles a liberal state because its aim is to permit the greatest range of human liberty consistent with peace. Hobbes stated the principle of this in his famous reformulation of the golden rule: "Do not that to another, which thou wouldest not have done to thyself." Not: *do* unto others as you would have them *do* to you. But: do *not* do as you would *not* have done. Leave your neighbor alone in exchange for his promise to leave you alone. The job of sovereign is to enforce that promise, and to guard against foreign enemies, and to do nothing else.

Libertarians will recognize this; it is, after all, the prototype of their state: the state that leaves men alone. It is the state that does not get involved in censorship, in moral education. It would not forbid abortions. It makes no attempt to form the character of its citizens. It takes men as they are. It does not preach. It does not attempt to make good Samaritans of travelers on the road from Jerusalem to Jericho, or New York to Washington, being content to provide highway police patrols as a way of protecting those travelers. It is the state built on the solid principle of self-interest. Men will obey the law, or live up to their contractual promise to leave other men alone, because it is in their interest to do so. If they do not, they will be punished by Leviathan. In short, this is the prototype of the "night watchman" state.

Some time ago, a leading libertarian spokesman honored the American Enterprise Institute by agreeing to speak on these subjects and to answer questions. He spoke of how in primitive societies there was a spirit of altruism, and of how the progress of civilization could be characterized by the gradual replacement of this altruism by self-interest. One of the questions he was asked was this: what if people, who have been taught to think first of themselves, or perhaps only of themselves, do not obey the laws (meaning, primarily, the criminal laws). His reply was, as one might expect, they will be punished. To which I now in turn reply: they will be punished *if* they are caught, and *if* the police and prosecutors are not corrupt, and *if* the society is not seduced by a compassion for criminals that causes them to pity the criminals and, in the extreme case (of which we have many examples) to blame their victims. What is our situation in the United States right now? Of the millions of FBI index crimes committed annually, 98.3 percent go unpunished.

That statistic alone is sufficient to demonstrate the foolishness of the libertarian argument. We live in a state profoundly influenced by Hobbesian principles, and a state that still employs a police force. But the radical (or extreme) libertarians would do away with the police force. They are Hobbesians without Leviathan. They would substitute private police forces. But why, on the basis of their own principles, should the private police forces, however well paid they are, protect their employers? I said earlier that the libertarians were Hobbesians but with a difference, and that this difference was of some magnitude. By advocating this abolition of public authority and its replacement by private arrangements, they are advocating, Hobbes would say, a return to the state of nature. What reason have they for thinking this state of nature will not be a state of war of everyman against everyman? Who among them has done the studies proving Hobbes was wrong about the nature of man? Or, why this confidence that the "spontaneous society" will be a decent society?

In 1764, a man who can fairly be described as the first criminologist, Cesare Beccaria, published what is surely the most influential criminal law book ever written, *Of Crimes and Punishments*. Beccaria was the first man to apply Hobbes' general principles to the specific subject of crime and punishment. He called for a massive decriminalization—to use our term for it—and enlightenment, and a vigorous enforcement of the criminal laws. Men were not to be morally educated—that part of the state was to wither away—but Beccaria was confident that they could be made to obey the criminal law out of self-interest: enlightenment will remind them of the terrors of the state of nature (and the terrible consequences if it were to return), and the threat of punishment will demonstrate to them the advantages of obeying the law. Would this system work? (And will libertarianism work?) Exactly one hundred years ago, Dostoevsky, in his *Notes from Underground*, ridiculed the very idea of it:

> But these were all golden dreams. Oh, tell me, who was it first announced, who was it first proclaimed that man only does nasty things because he does not know his own interests; and that if he were enlightened, if his eyes were open to his real normal interests, man would at once cease to do nasty things, would at once become good and noble because enlightened and understanding his real advantage, he would see his own advantage in the good and nothing else, and we all know that no one can, consciously, act against his own interests, consequently, so to say, through necessity, he would begin doing good? Oh, the babe! Oh, the pure innocent child!

One hundred years before Dostoevsky—in fact, even as Beccaria was writing—Rousseau ridiculed this Hobbesian and Beccarian idea of relying solely on self-interest. Will it not be likely, he asked, that if the laws are based merely on self-interest, some wicked men will see immediately that their interests can best be advanced if others obey the rule—he meant, Hobbes' reformulated golden rule, do *not* do as you would *not* be done to—while they disobey it? Rousseau thought so. And was he not right? He said that the wicked man will profit two ways: from the good man's justice and from his own injustice. In fact, the wicked man will be delighted if everyone, everyone except himself, obeys that rule.

To repeat: the question to be answered by the libertarians is this: what will be the effect of a system of law that says *only* that it is not in the interest of a man to commit a crime? Rousseau's answer was: there will be more crime. There will be more crime because once people are not governed by decent habits instilled in them with the assistance of the law, "they will soon enough discover the secret of how to evade the laws" (*Narcisse, ou L'Amant de lui-même*, Preface).

Rousseau was commenting on the Hobbesian state. It is not difficult to imagine what he would say about the libertarian version of the Hobbesian state, the Hobbesian state without Leviathan.

This country was officially founded on the principle of self-interest. "To secure these rights," says the Declaration of Independence, and these rights are private rights, "governments are instituted among men." Men institute government for selfish reasons. That was, and is, the principle on which we built. But, of course, the "we" who build on this principle were not simply self-interested men, not simply Hobbesian or Lockean men. We were, to an overwhelming extent, civilized Englishmen or British-men. We were not essentially *private* men: we were united in families, in churches, in towns and a host of other institutions. We were men whose habits had been acquired from a civilized past, whose character had been formed under the laws of an older and civilized politics. Moreover, while the national government did nothing in this area, the states, through their laws, continued to support the private institutions—the churches, the families—whose job it was to generate good moral habits. The states also provided a public education that was designed in large part to provide sound moral training. The states did not hesitate to act as censor.

I think what I have said above is sufficient to illustrate my point: we were founded on liberal principles, but we used the public authority in nonliberal ways. We did so partly out of habit, I suppose, and partly because there were men—Horace Mann, the central figure in American public schooling, is a good example—who reflected on our situation and who knew that a liberal state could not be perpetuated with simply self-interested citizens. Men had to be taught to be public-spirited, to care for others, to be at least somewhat altruistic.

In the course of time, and partly as the result of Supreme Court decisions affecting public education, public support of private education, and, of course, the censorship of obscenity, we have ceased to use the public authority in these ways. We can now be said to be living off the fat we built up in the past. I shudder to think of what would happen if we moved all the way from liberalism to libertarianism.

May I offer an anecdote: Several years ago, for a period of several years, I served on the advisory board of the National Institute of Law Enforcement and Criminal Justice. One of the subjects frequently discussed was the cause of crime. "Why do people commit crimes?" was the way the question was formulated. At one meeting I asked my colleagues on the Board, and the heads of the agency, and the Deputy Attorney General of the United States, who was also present, "why *not* commit crimes?" No one answered.

No one said, because it is wrong to commit a crime. I suspect they did believe it was wrong to commit a crime, but being sophisticated, no one felt free to answer in this simple but honest way. Their embarrassment speaks volumes to me. That embarrassment is one step away from the point where, when it is to their advantage to do so, they *will* commit crimes. Then we, and especially the libertarians among us, will have greater reason than ever to understand the point of Juvenal's familiar question, *sed quis custodiet ipsos custodes?*

Conservatism and Libertarianism

RICHARD M. WEAVER

The subject of this paper is the common ground between conservatism and libertarianism—not *possible* common ground, for I am convinced that they already, or naturally, share the same place on the political arc even though sometimes they are found eyeing one another rather uneasily. Among the theorists in both groups, it is true, we sometimes sense an unwillingness to come into a common front, apparently out of a feeling that this would require some fatal concessions. I hope to show that this is not so. It can be demonstrated that while the position of the conservative and that of the libertarian may not overlap exactly, they do have an overlapping and they certainly are not in necessary conflict.

The modifier which has been most frequently applied to my own writings is "conservative." I have not exactly courted this but I certainly have not resented it, and if I had to make a choice among the various appellations that are available, this is very likely the one that I would wind up with. I must say that I do not see any harm in it, and in this

I am unlike some of my friends, unlike some people with whom I agree on principles, but who appear to think that the term is loaded with unfavorable meanings or at least connotations.

And there is, in fact, a concept of conservatism filled with disagreement which needs to be fought by everyone who believes that a conservative philosophy is useful and constructive. There are some people who appear to think that conservatism means simply lack of imagination. The conservative, unable to visualize anything else, just wants to sit down with the status quo. There are others who seem to think that conservatism means timidity. The conservative is a person who has a sneaking presentiment that things might be better but he is simply afraid to take the risk of improvement. There are some who seem to think that conservatism is a product of temperamental slowness. If your mind or reflexes don't work as fast as other people's, then you must be a conservative. In these conceptions, the conservative is always found behind, whether from mental or physical deficiency, or just plain fearfulness. Naturally nobody looks to that kind of person for leadership.

But this is very far from my image of the conservative. A conservative in my view is a man who may be behind the times or up with the times or ahead of the times. It all depends on how you define the times. And this brings us at once to the matter of an essential definition.

> It is my contention that a conservative is a realist, who believes that there is a structure of reality independent of his own will and desire. He believes that there is a creation which was here before him, which exists now not by just his sufferance, and which will

be here after he's gone. This structure consists not merely of the great physical world but also of many laws, principles and regulations which control human behavior. Though this reality is independent of the individual, it is not hostile to him. It is in fact amenable by him in many ways, but it cannot be changed radically and arbitrarily. This is the cardinal point. The conservative holds that man in this world cannot make his will his law without any regard to limits and to the fixed nature of things.

There is in Elizabethan literature a famous poem entitled "A Mirror for Magistrates." It contains stories of a large number of rulers, kings, princes and others, who got into trouble and came to untimely and tragic ends. The story from these that I remember with special vividness concludes with this observation as a moral—and it is a kind of refrain line throughout the account: "He made his will his law." And that has stayed with me as a kind of description of the radical: he makes his will the law, instead of following the rules of justice and prudence. Fancying that his dream or wish can be substituted for the great world of reality, he gets into a fix from which some good conservative has to rescue him. The conservative I therefore see as standing on *terra firma* of antecedent reality; having accepted some things as given, lasting, and good, he is in a position to use his effort where effort will produce solid results.

Radicals and liberals sometimes try to knock the conservative off balance by asking, "What do you want to conserve anyhow?" I regard this question as by now substantially answered. The conservative wants to conserve the great structural reality which has been given us and which is on the whole beneficent.

I might make this a little more precise by saying he wants to respect it, although of course respect must carry with it the idea of conserving. There is a famous saying of Francis Bacon which can be applied with meaning here. Bacon does not seem the most likely figure to be brought into a defense of conservatism, but then every great thinker will say some things of general truth. Bacon declared that man learns to command nature by obeying her.

The same holds for the moral, social, and political worlds. One does not command these by simply trying to kick them over. One commands them as far as it is possible to do so or appropriate to do so by obeying them—by taking due note of their laws and regulations and by following these and then proceeding to further ends. Of course, the conservative does not accept everything that is as both right and unchangeable. That is contrary to the very law of life, but the changes that he makes are regardful of the forms that antedate, over-arch, and include him. The progress that he makes, therefore, is not something that will be undone as soon as his back is turned.

The attitude of the radical toward the real order is contemptuous, not to say contumacious. It is a very pervasive idea in radical thinking that nothing can be superior to man. This accounts, of course, for his usual indifference or hostility toward religion and it accounts also for his impatience with existing human institutions. His attitude is that anything man wants he both can and shall have, and impediments in the way are regarded as either accidents or affronts.

This is very easy to show from the language he habitually uses. He is a great scorner of the past and is always living in or for the future. Now since the future can never be anything more than one's subjective projection and since he affirmed that he believes only in the future, we are quite justified in saying that the radical lives in a world of fancy. Whatever of the present does not accord with his notions he classifies as "belonging to the past," and this will be done away with as soon as he and his party can get around to it. Whereas the conservative takes his lesson from a past that has objectified itself, the radical takes his from cues out of a future that is really the product of wishful thinking.

As a general rule, I am opposed to psychoanalyzing the opposition, knowing that this is a game both sides can play. But here we have a case so palpable that one is tempted to make an exception. So many of these radicals seem to be persons of disordered personality. There is something suspicious about this impassioned altruism. They often seem to be struggling to cover up some deep inner lack by trying to reform the habits or institutions of people thousands of miles away. Something like this becomes thus an obsession, almost to the point—or maybe to the point—of irrationality. Not that I regard all desire to reform the world as a sign of being crazy. Even more than that I would go along with Plato and say that some forms of craziness may be divinely inspired. But here we come to an essential distinction, and a parting of the ways. There is a difference between trying to reform your fellow beings by the normal processes of logical demonstration, appeal, and moral suasion—there is a difference between that and passing over to the use of force or constraint. The former is something all of us engage in every day. The latter is what makes the modern radical dangerous and perhaps in a sense demented. His first thought now is to get control of the state to make all men equal or to make all men rich, or failing that to make all men equally unhappy. This use of political instrumentality to coerce people to conform with his dream, in the face of their belief in a real order, is our reason, I think, for objecting to the radical. As an individual he may think about molding the world to his heart's desire. He may even publish the results of his thinking. But when he tries to use the instrumentality of the state to bring about his wishes then all of us are involved, and we have to take our stand.

Here, as I see it, is where conservatives and libertarians can stand on common ground. The libertarian, if my impression is correct, is a person who is interested chiefly in "freedom from." He is interested in setting sharp bounds to the authority of the state or other political forms over the individual. The right of the individual to an inviolable area of freedom as large as possible is thus his main concern. Libertarianism defined in this way is not as broad a philosophy as I conceive conservatism to be. It is narrower in purview and it is essentially negative, but this negative aspect is its very virtue.

It took the study of John Calhoun to wake me up to a realization that a constitution is and should be primarily a negative document. A constitution—and we may think primarily of the Constitution of the United States in this connection—is more to be revered for what it prohibits than for what it authorizes. A constitution is a series of "thou shalt nots" to the government, specifying the ways in which the liberties of individuals and of groups are not to be invaded. A constitution is a protection against that kind of arbitrary interference to which government left to itself is prone. It is right therefore to refer to our Constitution as a charter of liberties through its negative provisions, and it is no accident that in our day the friends of liberty have been pleaders for constitutional government. I think conservatives and libertarians stand together in being this kind of constitutionalist. Both want a settled code of freedom for the individual.

This is a shared *political* position, but we can show that their agreement has a philosophical basis. Both of them believe that there is an order of things which will largely take care of itself if you leave it alone. There are operating laws in nature and in human nature which are best not interfered with or not interfered with very much. If you try to change or suspend them by government fiat, the cost is greater than the return, the disorganization is expensive, the ensuing frustration painful. These laws are part of what I earlier referred to as the structure of reality. Just as there are certain conditions of efficiency for operations in the physical world, so there are conditions for efficient operation in the social and economic worlds.

There is a concept expressed by some economists today in the word "praxeology." Praxeology, briefly defined, is the science of how things work because of their essential natures. We find this out not by consulting our wishes but by observing *them*. For example, I believe it is a praxeological law that a seller will always try to get as much as he can for what he has to sell, and a buyer will always try to pay as little as he can to get it. That is a law so universal that we think of it as part of the order of things. Not only is this law a reliable index of human behavior; it also makes possible the free market economy, with its extremely important contribution to political freedom.

The conservative and the libertarian agree that it is not only presumption, it is folly to try to interfere with the workings of a praxeology. One makes use of it, yes, in the same way that a follower of Bacon makes use of nature by obeying her. The great difference is that one is recognizing the objective; one is recognizing the laws that regulate man's affairs. Since the conservative and libertarian believe that these cannot be wished away through the establishment of a Utopia, they are both conservators of the real world.

My instincts are libertarian, and I am sure that I would never have joined effort with the conservatives if I had not been convinced that they are the defenders of freedom today. This fact is so evident in the contemporary world that one hardly needs to point out examples of it.

It requires only a little experience in politics or publishing for one to learn that the enemies of freedom today are the radicals and the militant liberals. Not only do they propose through their reforms to reconstruct and regiment us, they also propose to keep us from hearing the other side. Anyone who has contended with Marxists and their first cousins, the totalitarian liberals, knows that they have no intention of giving the conservative alternative a chance to compete with their doctrines for popular acceptance. If by some accident they are compelled physically to listen, it is with indifference or a contempt because they really consider the matter a closed question—that is, no longer on the agenda of discussable things.

The conservative, on the other hand, is tolerant because he has something to tolerate from, because he has in a sense squared himself with the structure of reality. Since his position does not depend upon fiat and wishfullness, he does not have to be nervously defensive about it. A new idea or an opposing idea is not going to topple his. He is accordingly a much fairer man and I think a much more humane man than his opposite whom I have been characterizing. He doesn't feel that terrible need to exterminate the enemy which seems to inflame so many radicals of both the past and the present.

This can be shown by relating an incident from the career of George Washington, who figures in my mind as the archetypal American conservative—a man versed in the ways of the world but uncorrupted by them, a man whose unshakable realism saved our infant republic. Washington, for example, had the very ticklish job—of maintaining relations with radical, revolutionary France during both of his administrations. In 1789 there arrived in this country one Citizen Genet, new minister from the French Republic, whose commission it really was to stir up trouble. He tried to involve the United States in a new war with Great Britain, and he even threatened to appeal to the American people over the head of their government. He was the sharpest thorn in Washington's side for some while.

But the next year, 1794, came the fall of Genet's party, the Gironde, and the accession to power of Robespierre and his radical Jacobin government. Genet was replaced, and Washington was requested to send him back to France, where he undoubtedly would have faced the guillotine. But, and I here quote the words of a recent biographer: "Washington would take no agency, even remote, in the bloody business of the French terror, whatever Genet had done or tried to do, the president did not intend to order the young man to his doom. If Genet wished, it was agreed, he might have political asylum in America." So Genet became an American citizen and lived peacefully for forty years in our conservative republic. This impresses me as a classical instance of conservative tolerance and essential humaneness.

But thinking back to this period may remind us that Washington was himself a revolutionist, and this to my mind refutes any notion that a conservative must be distinguished by timidity and apathy. When the time is out of joint, he can be an active exponent of change. The difference is that he does not have the inflamed zeal of his counterpart, the radical revolutionist, who thinks that he must cut off the heads of his opponents because he cannot be objective about his own frustrations. It is interesting to know in taking leave of this subject that Washington's Farewell Address was noticed by the London *Times*. What it had to say was this: "General Washington's address is the most complete comment upon English Clubs and Clubbists, upon factions and parties and factious partisans. The authority of this revolutionist may be set up against the wild and wicked revolutionists of Europe, if not as an altar against an altar at least as an altar against sacrilege."

In conclusion, I maintain that the conservative in his proper character and role is a defender of liberty. He is such because he takes his stand on the real order of things and because he has a very modest estimate of man's ability to change that order through the coercive power of the state.

He is prepared to tolerate diversity of life and opinion because he knows that not all things are of his making and that it is right within reason to let each follow the law of its own being. A rigid equalitarianism is to him unthinkable because he appreciates that truth so well expressed by the poet Blake: "One law for the lion and the ox is oppression." I therefore can see nothing to keep him from joining hands with the libertarian, who arrives at the same position by a different route, perhaps, but out of the same impulse to condemn arbitrary power.

Conservatism and Libertarianism: Vital Complements

JOHN P. EAST

As the American conservative movement of the post-World War II era passes its fiftieth year, it appears not only appropriate but essential to evaluate thoroughly its theoretical base. The movement is composed of traditional and libertarian emphases. Frequently, these respective facets seem symbiotic, if not completely compatible, yet on occasion these two perspectives appear distinct, separate, and irreconcilable. Historically, this loose alliance has been an uneasy one, and a perspective of over fifty years offers a unique opportunity for reevaluation.

The traditional emphasis is preoccupied with value, purpose, meaning, and ends. Although it deeply reveres freedom, it anguishes even more over the absence of virtue in individuals and society, and the failure to pursue the ethically and morally correct. Moreover, while it acknowledges the importance of rights (and even demands on occasion), the traditional view is more enamored of the theoretical imperatives of duty, obligation, and service.

And while appreciative of the vital role of individualism in the Western heritage, the traditionalist is more distressed by the presence of anomie and the absence of community in modern mass society.

Traditionalism draws its theoretical sustenance from classical Greek, particularly Platonic, and biblical roots. There is an abiding sense of transcendence—"the pull of the Golden Cord," as Eric Voegelin defined it, or "the character of ascent" as described by Leo Strauss. The Creator has ordained the order of being, and in this divinely established order things have their innate and unchangeable natures. In sum, man is not self-produced, nor is his fundamental nature malleable. Thinking man is constantly reminded of his creatureliness, of his dependence, and of his frailty and finiteness. In view of the majesty and mystery of creation, reverence and awe suggest the appropriate mood. Piety is the preeminent virtue, and the perennial task of man is to discern the natural and moral parameters of his existence and to attune himself accordingly. The intellectual inspirers of traditionalist thought are Plato, Cicero, Augustine, Burke, and others of comparable stature and substance.

To the traditionalist, the major weaknesses in modern thought are traceable most directly to the Renaissance and the Enlightenment. In these areas secularism emerged as the dominant theme; man thought of himself as self-produced and self-defining; and man became the center and measure of all being. There was enormous confidence in reason and science; hence, there was inordinate confidence in man. At best, modern thought became shallow and thin; too often, it was unabashedly egotistical, leading to impiety (the greatest of intellectual heresies), with the potential for unchecked degeneracy. In Western thought, the traditionalists conceive their principal philosophical opponents as being Machiavelli, Hobbes, Locke, Rousseau, Voltaire, Bentham, Comte, Hegel, Mill, Marx, and Nietzsche, and the isms these thinkers spawned: totalitarianism, authoritarianism, hedonism, fanaticism, atheism, utilitarianism, positivism, statism, relativism, egalitarianism, and nihilism. These isms are the icons of the modern age. As different as these thinkers and their respective rationales appear to be, there are the common denominators of secularism, man-centeredness, and the insatiable quest for earthly utopias of human design. Impiety is the cardinal theoretical weakness, and to the traditionalists it is the fatal flaw of modern thought. In terms of substance of thought and weight of impact, the preeminent traditional theorists would include Willmoore Kendall, Richard Weaver, Leo Strauss, Eric Voegelin, and Russell Kirk.

The libertarian dimension of conservative thinking, though by no means invariably agnostic or atheistic, exhibits a more secular cast in its theoretical approach. It places considerable confidence in the capacity of reason and science to produce unending progress. Sanguine about the creative and productive capacity of man, libertarians are powerful exponents of individualism, freedom, private property, the division of labor, and of the capacity of the spontaneous forces of the free market to utilize and maximize human creative and productive potential. Less concerned about absolutes and particular ends, libertarians are strongly committed to maintaining the procedures and mechanisms of the free and open society. That is, the values and goals of specific individuals or societies are of less consequence than the maintenance of the apparatus of the free society. On ends libertarianism is relativistic, on the elements of freedom it is highly principled. The philosophical roots of libertarianism are found in such diverse figures as Adam Smith, John Locke, Thomas Jefferson, Frederic Bastiat, Lord Acton, Hilaire Belloc, John Stuart Mill (at least the Mill of *On Liberty* fame), and Karl Popper. Beneath their considerable diversity as thinkers, these writers did concur on the virtues of reason, individualism, and the limited state. With differing emphases and rationales, each contributed to the grammar of freedom as reflected in libertarian thought.

The philosophical enemies of libertarianism would include all forms of collectivism, whether it be the Ideal State of Plato, the nationalism of Machiavelli, the authoritarianism of Hobbes, the statism of Hegel, the totalitarianism of Marx, the socialist egalitarianism of the Fabians, or the more genteel welfare statism of the Keynesians. In addition, some libertarians (Friedrich von Hayek is a notable exception) are uncomfortable with the Burkean emphasis upon community, the traditional, and the organic, for these concepts, like the harsher collectivisms, suggest the subordination of the free, autonomous individual to higher movements or systems. Finally, the secular bent of libertarianism makes it suspect and skeptical of religion. At best, religion is often too dependent on emotion rather than on reason, and its epistemology is too dependent upon the mystical and obscure. Religion lacks the empirical and quantitative nature of reason and science; hence, its intellectual nature is frequently less probing and demanding, and the quality of its findings less certain and reliable. At its worst, the libertarian sees religion in its more fervent forms evolving into religiosity and ultimately taking on an anti-intellectual and potentially authoritarian cast. Religion then becomes merely another collectivism with hostility to reason, individualism, the limited state, and free choice. As measured by their impact upon and acceptance by the mainstream of American conservative thought, the preeminent spokesmen for libertarian values would be Ludwig von Mises and his famous pupil, Friedrich von Hayek.

The traditionalist and libertarian elements of the American conservative movement do reveal some areas of theoretical compatibility. Most conspicuous in this regard is the central role of the concept of the individual. While the traditionalist may stress the moral and ethical obligations of the individual, and while the libertarian may emphasize individual rights, both agree on the vital and controlling concept involving the dignity and worth of the person. Moreover, there would be unity in opposition to the egalitarian-collectivist bent of the modern age, whether that bent be reflected in authoritarianism, totalitarianism, or any other variant of contemporary statism. These isms agree in seeking to subordinate and submerge the individual into a molded and manipulated whole, and this end is abhorrent to all facets of American conservative thought.

There are, however, areas of apparent theoretical incompatibility. Libertarianism is strongly utilitarian and relativistic in its theoretical commitment. It despairs of our ever knowing the ultimate moral and ethical first principles; that is, of ever knowing the truth, and hence it is indifferent, if not on occasion hostile, to the Platonic and biblical theoretical contributions to the Western heritage. In this disavowal of Platonic and biblical roots, libertarians clearly break with traditionalist views. Indeed, in the case of the latter, the classical Greek and biblical origins are the primary foundations of the Western experience. This difference presents a theoretical cleavage of substantial proportions.

More subtle, but of some consequence, is that theoretical difference pertaining to the Burkean view. In an age of unbridled egoism, narcissism, and acute obsession with the significance of the contemporaneous, traditionalists argue the value of that perspective offering a sense of history, tradition, and community. As the traditionalist sees it, libertarianism, by elevating the clamor for individual rights and demands to the theoretical first principle, comes perilously close to making the unrestrained individual ego its philosophical centerpiece, and thereby runs the risk of ensconcing pride, and hence impiety, as the guiding principle of Western thought. From the traditionalist view, which draws heavily from the classical and biblical heritages, impiety, of course, is the ultimate philosophical error, for it leads to a philosophy of anti-philosophy. The philosopher is no longer to pursue understanding of the world and to attune himself to it; rather, he is to change it to conform to his heady vision of what it ought to be; that is, he is to gain dominion over being. The philosopher is at once ideologue and utopian. This view is repugnant to the traditionalist mind, and it suggests a theoretical fissure of some consequence between the respective spheres of American conservative thought. The Burkean vantage point, which traditionalists find highly pertinent in this context, reminds one of the frailty and finiteness of the ill-conceived autonomous individual, and informs one of the shallowness and error in failing to understand the enormous limitations and dependence of individual man, which are brought into sharp relief by an appreciation of community, tradition, and history.

Indeed, some conservatives of the traditionalist persuasion fear that certain dominant forces in contemporary American libertarianism have gone beyond the mature and balanced libertarian thought of Mises, Hayek, and their students and have taken on the character of a hardened ideology. According to these critics, the problem stems from the common philosophical error of taking a valid point, in this case the importance of the individual and his rights, and elevating it to the first principle of life with all other considerations excluded. When a fragment of the truth is wrenched out of the context of the whole and made the sole preoccupation of the philosopher, there is the imminent danger of converting the philosopher into ideologue and philosophy into ideology. Where genuine libertarianism is committed to the legitimate role of the limited state in protecting against internal and external disorders, and in adjudicating disputes among its citizens, the new ideological libertarianism is anti-state and seems bent on excursions into the mindless, chaotic, and disoriented world of anarchy. In view of the social nature of man (Aristotle had artfully instructed the Western mind on that point), regarding the conduct of domestic affairs, traditional conservatives find the new libertarianism naive and simplistic; in view of the ominous realities of foreign affairs in an age that continues to be harried by totalitarian dictatorship and terrorist revolutionaries, the traditionalists find the new libertarians not only appallingly ill-informed but incredibly foolish. Thus, as between the traditional conservatives and the new libertarians, a philosophical and practical chasm of the first order has emerged.

Among the preeminent thinkers of American conservative thought, the late Frank S. Meyer made the most concerted effort to weave together into an American conservative philosophy the diverse strands of traditional and libertarian thought. Meyer did not approach his task in the role of arbitrator or compromiser, nor did he attempt to force an unnatural union of irreconcilables; rather, he articulated a conservative philosophy of a most principled form. To Meyer, in the Western experience, whether one is emphasizing rights or duties and obligations, it is the symbol of the Incarnation which establishes the individual permanently and irrevocably "as the ordering principle, the fount and end of social being." Indisputably, Meyer is a Christian theorist, and the Christian faith is the *summum bonum* of his thinking. All of his other ideas flow from that fact and are corollaries to it.

Meyer utilized libertarian and traditionalist strains of thought to the degree that each strain contributed to the realization of his ultimate political idea. Traditionalism was useful to the extent it reminded one of the supreme importance of value, meaning, goals, and ultimately of transcendent purpose. In sum, it instructed one on the character of the virtuous life—the highest calling for the individual and society. Libertarianism was valuable for the lessons it offered on the grammar and structure of freedom. Meyer observed, "[This] double allegiance to virtue and to freedom is the over-all consensus of contemporary American conservatism..." and the "love of liberty and the love of truth are not the hostile standards of irreconcilable parties; rather, they form together the twin sign of any viable conservatism." Thus, traditionalism, with its emphasis upon virtue, and libertarianism, in its preoccupation with freedom, were the vital strands in the fabric of American conservative thought. Meyer concluded, "*virtue in freedom*—this is the goal of our endeavor."

Meyer rejected those elements of traditionalism and libertarianism which interfered with the realization of the first principle of American conservatism: the free man seeking Christian virtue in a community of limited government. In its fascination with heritage and authority, traditionalism sometimes erred. The idolization of heritage and tradition could not be an end in and of itself, for that would lead not to a principled conservatism, but merely to a blind obedience to that which is inherited, to little more than primitive ancestor worship. Nor, as Meyer viewed it, did traditionalism contribute to a legitimate American conservatism to the extent it became overly enamoured of employing public or private authority to coerce virtue. For an action to be virtuous, Meyer contended, it had to be freely chosen. Coerced virtue was a contradiction in terms, and on occasion traditionalism contributed to that theoretical confusion. Meyer warned that traditionalism was frequently "far too ready to subordinate the individual person to the authority of state or society."

In its preoccupation with freedom, libertarianism revealed a theoretical weakness wherein it lowered and

narrowed its sights and made liberty its sole concern.
Meyer explained:

> The place of freedom in the spiritual economy of men
> is a high one indeed, but it is specific and not absolute.
> By its very nature, it cannot be an end of men's
> existence. Its meaning is essentially freedom from
> coercion, but that, important as it is, cannot be an
> end. It is empty of goal or norm. Its function is to
> relieve men of external coercion so that they may
> freely seek their good.

On another occasion, he cautioned, "Free individualism
uninformed by moral value rots at its core and soon
surrenders to tyranny." Hence to the degree that libertarians had no interest in or no conception of an objective
moral order, they exposed their most critical theoretical
deficiency.

Frank Meyer offered the most substantive and enduring
effort of "fusionism" (Brent Bozell's term), and in scan-
ning the forty years of the American conservative movement his analysis still serves as the indispensable point of
departure in evaluating the contemporary status of that
event. His contribution allows an examination of the
current state of American conservative thought to commence with a firm foundation, for he raises the vital
questions of compatibility and incompatibility between the
dominant themes of conservative thinking. Moreover, and
quite significantly, there is little doubt that Meyer would be
deeply troubled with a metamorphosis in the conservative
movement whereby an ideological libertarianism became
the dominant and controlling element. In Meyer's thought,

libertarianism was clearly a part of the whole, but to subtly convert it into the whole would be a grievous philosophical error. The search for the good life, according to Meyer, must commence with the pursuit of virtue, with that which is morally and ethically correct, and freedom, though a vital supplement to that pursuit, is not a substitute for it.

The potential for a broadbased conservatism, composed of traditional and libertarian emphases, remains. If traditionalists and libertarians agree on the crucial matters of individualism and anti-collectivism, and if, as Meyer contended, traditionalism and libertarianism, in spite of differences, remain vital complements, then optimism concerning a viable and effective American conservative movement is warranted. Of course, there will remain areas of troublesome conflict triggered by extreme posturings from various quarters, yet the petulance of a few need not be allowed to abort the task of forging a conservative vital center. The function of this vital center is to identify and conserve the theoretical best in the Western heritage.

Toward a New
Intellectual History

M. Stanton Evans

In offering this essay I feel at once ambitious and diffident: ambitious because the task of rewriting Western intellectual history is a project of enormous significance and scope; diffident because such a task is far beyond my meager powers. I should therefore like to stress at the outset that the rewriting to which I refer has been—and is being—done by others, not by me. What I shall have to say derives from the researches of Maitland, Von Gierke, and Figgis in the nineteenth century, and Frankfort, Dawson, Bloch and numerous others in our own.

The burden of my argument is that, in discussions of the theoretical reconciliation of conservatism and libertarianism, the word "fusion" is a misnomer. It suggests that, in combining traditionalist and libertarian emphases, we are yoking together disparate elements. I would argue instead that we are describing a natural and necessary unity, and that it is the separation of these emphases that is unnatural and mistaken. It would be possible to show this, I believe, by a thematic reconciliation of the points at issue—to argue that a libertarian regime is better established on traditionalist assumptions about the nature of man, political power, and virtue, than on utilitarian or classical liberal assumptions; that a traditionalist ethic will ultimately require a libertarian social policy, and so on.

However, my approach in this essay will be historical rather than thematic. I shall argue that the unnatural separation of traditionalist and libertarian emphases occurs because of the way we have been taught our intellectual history. In the usual construction, it is assumed that the distinctive elements of modern Western society—scientific progress, democratic government, individual liberty, etc.—have been achieved by throwing off the religious traditions of the Christian Middle Ages, which are usually depicted as a time of intellectual somnolence, stagnation of commerce and political repression.

That the facts of the case are rather different is something we are beginning to discover as a number of scholars have set about to reconstruct our intellectual genealogy. I think it can be shown that individual liberty, limited government, representative institutions and the scientific attainments of the West are products of Biblical theism generally, and of the Christian Middle Ages in particular. To appreciate this perspective, it is necessary to reverse the usual tenets of economic and technological determinism, which hold that material forces somehow dictate political relations, ethical values and religious sentiments. What I am suggesting instead is a theological determinism; which is to say that theology determines metaphysics, which determines political philosophy and institutions, which in turn determine the economic and technological organization of society.

From this standpoint the decisive development in the emergence of Western culture and its distinctive ethical, political and intellectual values is the advent of Biblical theism. Numerous elements from classical antiquity, Teutonic tribal custom and adventitious circumstances of European political conflict were melded into the final product, but the controlling and integrating principles were those derived from Biblical theism. As Frankfort, Eliade and others have instructed us, the polytheisms of antiquity assumed an ultimate divinity in nature. Gods of the sea, the river, the forest, the harvest, were to be feared, entreated and propitiated. To conduct these functions—to serve as "intermediary between humanity and the powers in nature," as Frankfort puts it—was the principal job of the pharaoh, king, or other political authority.

Theologies of this type, whatever their other variations, had a number of traits in common. Most notably, they held man in subjection to nature and its recurrent cycles; they were essentially magical in character; and they viewed the state as a religious institution as well as a political one. Under such conditions, Western notions of individual freedom, limited government, and scientific progress could scarcely be imagined. The political state had a total lien on the energies and affections of the citizen. Nature was a cockpit of capricious and often warring divinities, and knowledge of its workings was magical and esoteric.

As Voegelin has shown at length, various of the ancient philosophers attempted to break past these barriers, and in some cases came close to doing so, albeit with attendant difficulties. But with the advent of Biblical monotheism, the intellectual landscape was suddenly and drastically transformed. It was this transformation which, above all else, was responsible for the development of Western society and its distinctive mind-set. In the Biblical perspective, God is the Creator of physical nature, but nature is not itself divine. There are no polytheistic deities of sea, wind, and harvest to be propitiated. Which means, among other things, that the political state no longer has this integrating function. The state exists within the providence of God, but its leaders now are charged, essentially, with keeping secular order. The political state is no longer capable of negotiating the final issues, no longer the unchallenged arbiter of divine intention in society.

As the political state is scaled down in the Biblical perspective, so the individual is raised up. In the Christian view, every person is precious because he or she is a child of God, made in His image. Every person has an immortal, individuated soul, and is embarked on a drama of existence which has as its central issue the question of personal salvation. The result is an intense psychological individualism, the basis, as Gilson has noted, of the Western idea of personality. Other aspects of the Biblical perspective are relevant also, but I shall mention only three: (1) the idea of Covenant between God and the people of Israel, prior to the advent of Kingship; (2) the affirmation of the reality and goodness of the created order, as the handiwork of God; (3) the notion of an intelligible harmony in the universe, replacing the form-matter dualisms of antiquity (which afflicted the philosophers as well).

Dawson, Bark and others have convincingly argued that

these notions provide the conceptual basis of Western society—its political institutions, its ideas of personal freedom, its science and its economic progress. From these beginnings we derive the precepts, contrary to the ancient view, that the king is *not* the law speaking; that the religious authorities—the prophets in the Old Testament era, the Church in the new era—are separate from the political state, and may render judgment on it; that political authority arises from consent of the governed, and so on. It is precisely in the Christian Middle Ages that these ideas develop in institutional form. The leading political idea of the medieval period was of course constitutionalism—that the king was under God, and the law. This is the famous theme of Bracton—and, retrospectively, of Fortescue and Lord Coke. Political power, moreover, was practically constrained by the authority of the Church—and also by the wide dispersion of economic and military power that characterized the medieval equilibrium.

The second leading idea of the period, I would venture to say, was that of contract. The much-maligned feudal system was in fact a network of contracts—in which political allegiance was based on the notion of reciprocity. If the lord did not fulfill his obligation to the vassal, then the vassal's allegiance was dissolved. Such ideas were congruent both with the notion of individual worth on both sides of the transaction, and with the Biblical idea of covenant. Also congruent with such notions, and dictated by the circumstances of the time, was the development of representative institutions. If we consult the Pipe Rolls recording the transactions of the early parliaments, we find kings affirming rights and privileges of their subjects as a necessary condition of obtaining revenue which they did not possess of their own authority. Hence the tight connection, in our tradition, between popular government and the question of taxation.

If it seems strange to think of the medieval period as a nursery of free institutions, we need only reflect that Magna Carta was a preeminently feudal document, imposed on the king by the barons and clergy. And, from the other direction, we may also reflect that it was the "reception" of Roman law at the time of the Renaissance which revived the authoritarian precept that "the king is the law speaking." In the medieval era, these libertarian ideas and practices existed in a kind of emulsion. As Maitland says, to understand the era and its ideas of the "given-ness" of political institutions, we must "think ourselves back into a twilight." It was the religious-political crisis of the Reformation which forced the articulation of these concepts in their modern form.

That crisis presented situations in which a monarch of one confession sought to impose his rule on a sizable number of his subjects who held the opposite opinion. This confronted the subjects with the necessity of justifying resistance to the monarch, and sent them back to the medieval and Biblical precedents. There they found the ideas of which we have been speaking: that the king is under God and the law, and must conduct himself accordingly; that the king, as a feudal sovereign, was reciprocally bound to provide his subjects with protection as a condition of their allegiance; and that the authority of kings, while ultimately of God, was on the Biblical record intermediately of the people.

All these ideas were forcefully brought forward, by Catholic and Protestant theoreticians alike, as religious conflicts sharpened in the sixteenth century. We find them most coherently expressed in the *Vindiciae Contra Tyrannos*—which is at once an intensely medieval and intensely modern document. (It is noteworthy that, when the *Vindiciae* was published in London, the common assumption was that it had been written by the Jesuits.) Such ideas were inevitably in conflict with the revived conception of expansive monarchy in which the work of the king was absolute law. The most relevant collision of these forces from our standpoint occurred in seventeenth-century England, as Stuart kings confronted tenacious Parliaments filled with devotees of medieval constitution-alism and Puritan squires steeped in the convenantal doctrines of resistance. The apex of this struggle was the Parliament of 1628, populated by pre-Cromwellian Puri-tans and Sir Edward Coke, the common law incarnate.

This was the Parliament that adopted the Petition of Right, stressing traditional immunities against arbitrary taxation and imprisonment, and the Three Resolves, again denouncing arbitrary taxes and demanding Calvinist or-thodoxy in the church. This Parliament represented the high-water mark of libertarian doctrine, derived from medieval sources, in the England of the seventeenth cen-tury. It was precisely at this phase of the proceedings that our own forefathers—intent on covenantal notions of church and civil government—departed England for these shores. They strongly objected to Laud's campaign to rule through bishops, and came to America to establish church and civil practice on congregational principles. They planted here not only the English common law but specific institutions of government derived from their medieval-feudal heritage and their covenantal theology.

In fact, these covenantal principles had already been partially established in Virginia, under the charter of 1618. This constitution was drawn up by Sir Edwin Sandys, son of a Puritan archbishop and traveler on the Continent when the *Vindiciae* was in fashion. Sandys had served on a parliamentary committee inquiring into the feudal prerogatives of the kings, and argued in the House of Commons in 1613 that the power of the monarch was exercised under "certain reciprocal conditions" which "neither king nor people could violate with impunity." Virginia under the Sandys charter, unsurprisingly, became the site of the first representative assembly in the new world, the House of Burgesses.

It was, however, in the New England colonies under the systematic Puritans that the implications of the medieval mind-set and covenantal theology achieved their greatest theoretical clarity. Again, as with feudalism, we must get past conventional stereotypes to understand the reality of the situation. While they were by no means modern libertarians and had no truck with religious toleration, the Puritans were anything but believers in unchecked authority. On the contrary, they were ardent constitutionalists, highly suspicious of arbitrary power. The characteristic Puritan view was stated by John Cotton, theologian-in-chief to Massachusetts Bay. "Let all the world," Cotton said, "learn to give mortal men no greater power than they are content they shall use, for use it they will.... It is necessary that all power that is on earth be limited, church-power or other.... It is considered a matter of great danger to the state to limit prerogatives, but it is a further danger not to have them limited."

Such opinions were dictated by the Puritans' pessimistic view of human nature and their heritage of Christian constitutionalism. The practices adopted in Massachusetts Bay were in keeping with this background. Thus, despite the fact that the Massachusetts Bay Company was a private corporation in which voting powers could have been restricted to the eight original members, the first meeting of the Massachusetts General Court in October 1630 was thrown open to the votes of 116 people—in accordance with congregational doctrine.

Other aspects of Massachusetts politics likewise reflected the influence of such principles: the strict separation of church and civil government (a minister could not hold political office); a strong emphasis on local town government; development of a bicameral legislature on checks-and-balances principles; and the adoption of the Body of Liberties—precursor to the Bill of Rights—in response to what was seen as the undue influence of Governor Winthrop. In these developments, we find the embryo of virtually all the political institutions which were embodied in the constitutions of the several states, and were transferred thence into the Constitution of the new American Republic. From this perspective, it is possible to see that the institutions of limited, representative government, far from being products of secular intuition, were derivative from our religious heritage generally and the political practices of the medieval era specifically. It is a conceit of modernity to suppose that these ideas were invented by the theoreticians of the Enlightenment.

A good example of this conceit is the usual treatment accorded the notion of "social contract." Most discussions of social contract assume the idea was invented by Locke, that it is a purely speculative, ahistorical concept, and that the American colonists imbibed the contractual principles expressed in the Declaration of Independence and other revolutionary documents from such sources. In response to these assertions, we need only note that—contrary to the usual statements on this subject—there *was* a society of historical record based explicitly on social contract: Plymouth Colony. The Mayflower Compact, which formed the basis of this polity, states "we do combine and covenant together to create a civil body politic..., etc."

In view of what has been said about the contractual nature of the feudal tie, the Biblical stress on covenant and the teachings of the *Vindiciae*, such an arrangement is hardly astonishing. Obviously, the Pilgrims got their social contract notions from such sources, not from Locke—who didn't publish his *Treatise on Civil Government* until 69 years later. (In fact, Locke derived his ideas about such matters from Hooker—who in turn derived them from the Christian-classical political tradition.) The social contract language of the American Revolution, as it appears in the Declaration and in the writings of Chief Justice Drayton, is of similar provenance. These formulations—that the king has withdrawn his protection and is no longer owed allegiance—are eminently feudal and virtually identical in logic and phrasing to the *Vindiciae*.

The attribution of ideas derived from the Western religious heritage to the secularism of the Renaissance and

Enlightenment is equally mistaken in the realm of science, concerning which a brief footnote may be in order. As Stanley Jaki has recently argued in a series of brilliant books, the achievements of Western science, like the achievements of Western statecraft, may be traced to the influence of Biblical theism, which posits the reality and importance of the created order, and which rejects the cyclical assumptions and form-matter dualisms of the ancient cosmologies and philosophers.

In the Biblical perspective, as Jaki puts it, the universe is "a totality of interacting things," harmonious in character and intelligible to human reason, which is part of the same creation formed by the same creator. In this respect, it is noteworthy that Copernicus, Kepler and Galileo were all devout Christian theists, moved by an appreciation of the universal harmony in rejecting Aristotelian geocentrism. It is equally noteworthy that the Renaissance, with its revival of pagan ideas and practices, was famously hospitable to magic. The idea of a vast harmony with a multitude of interacting parts that gave birth to the Western conception of science is markedly similar, it should be added, to the idea of the market. In fact, it seems unlikely that market theory, envisioning the interaction of millions of transactions through the reconciling mechanism of a spontaneous order, could have arisen in any other cultural setting.

Even in a brief recapitulation, it should be evident that we have derived a host of political and social values from our religious heritage: personal freedom and individualism, limited government-constitutionalism and the order-keeping state, the balance and division of powers, separation of church and state, federalism and local autonomy, government by consent and representative institutions, bills of rights, and privileges. Add to these the development of Western science, the notion of progress over linear time, egalitarianism and the like, and it is apparent that the array of ideas and attitudes that we think of as characteristically secular and liberal are actually by-products of our religion. It may be said, indeed, that the characteristic feature of liberalism, broadly defined—classical as well as modern— has been an attempt to take these by-products, sever them from their theological origins, and make them independent and self-validating. On the whole, it has not been a totally successful experiment.

Let me stress, by way of conclusion, what I am *not* saying in these remarks. I am not suggesting that wherever Christianity has reigned, there has been free government in all its plenitude, or that Christians have always adhered to the principles derived from their tradition. Nor am I saying the secular by-products of Biblical faith may be taken as justifications for it. While these are good as far as they go, they are not the ultimate good, and the truths of religious faith are self-justifying.

What I am arguing, instead, is a kind of tautology: that the characteristic values and institutions of Western society have arisen and flourished only where the writ of Western religious faith has run—hardly an astonishing proposition unless one ignores the influence that religious belief, in one guise or another, exerts in the shaping of human cultures. It is in this context, I believe, that the central disputes between the traditionalists and libertarians among us may be resolved: our tradition is a tradition of freedom, and our libertarian precepts are undergirded by the traditional values of our faith.

Libertarianism:
The Principle of Liberty

Tibor R. Machan

In recent years the point of view or doctrine called libertarianism has come of age in more ways than one. There are now detailed and competently—sometimes brilliantly and wisely—developed theories supporting this position.[1] Numerous organizations—academic associations, lay societies, "think tanks," and a political party—compose the libertarian "movement."[2] Disputes, too, abound among those who would unhesitatingly identify themselves as libertarians.[3] Both systematic and off-hand attacks on libertarianism emanate from various intellectual, political, journalistic, social and other circles.[4] The opportunity to publish works discussing the positions pro and con now exists beyond the limited range of a few "in group" publishers.[5] Academic courses in politics and philosophy often cover the subject matter.[6] And the language of day to day politics now exhibits signs of the influence of libertarianism (as distinct from more traditional American political ideals).[7]

Libertarianism is to a considerable extent a theoretical extension of crucial concepts found in the American political tradition—e.g., liberty, consent, rights, equality, due process—so the position is not a radical challenge to the American tradition. (This may be disputed by some, of course, depending on whether they regard the American political tradition as distinctive in its libertarian or in some other elements.)[8] As such, libertarianism is properly associated with aspects of American conservatism. Many American conservatives cherish institutions and practices that reflect libertarian ideals or principles. So American conservatives are concerned with maintaining or supporting some institutions to which libertarianism gives theoretic support. In practical terms this has led to frequent coalitions between conservatives and libertarians—e.g., in their advocacy of the protection and preservation of the free market, defense of the institution of private property, support of a legal system that respects personal responsibility and places severe restrictions on the power of (at least the federal) government.[9]

Yet it is clear that often many conservatives are not comfortable with libertarianism despite agreements on some of the practical issues. Conservatives tend, on the whole, to be anti-rationalistic in their methodology.[10] Libertarians, in the main, have high regard for reason—for uncovering objective and true principles from which to derive subsidiary political and legal principles and infer various practical policy recommendations or prohibitions.[11] Some embrace an empiricist rationalism, some a Cartesian, and yet others an Aristotelian/Thomistic variety, but virtually all consider the reliance on the human mind and what it can discover about reality as something to be encouraged, not demeaned.[12]

More particularly, the principled adherence to individual liberty—e.g., the right of every individual to live by the judgments he or she makes and to be free from the imposition of others concerning his conduct affecting his life—has led libertarians to support resistance to all political and legal measures (in various ways, depending on circumstance) that aim at imposing upon human beings a way of life they individually reject.[13] Conservatives do not share, in the main, I contend, such a *principled* commitment to liberty and would refuse to apply this (putative) principle to many cases that a libertarian clearly would. Thus the latter would enjoin the regulation of entertainment by public authorities, even in cases deemed tasteless—e.g., "topless" dancing. Conservatives would consider such public policy permissible—at least at the community level.[14] Other examples abound, but in general, I would say, conservatives tend to deny any *principle* of liberty in the first place, and they would very likely dispute some of the basic aspects of libertarianism, including some crucial elements of arguments usually advanced in support of the doctrine.[15]

It is my aim to show in this essay that some of the points persistently raised by conservatives with respect to libertarianism can be met. For example, I will indicate that considerations of social morality and standards of community conduct are by no means ruled out for libertarians, who attend to them in a principled but voluntary manner. In this I will stress the point that political authority is ill suited for purposes of preserving and upgrading the moral climate of a human community. Libertarians contend that politicians are not moral leaders!

My aim is not to seek out the most extreme versions of conservative thought, nor to attempt to explain and justify the more bizarre renditions of "libertarianism" that some conservatives focus on in their scrutiny. Every point of view has its most implausible as well as its blandest versions, and an honest confrontation with it must avoid focusing on either of these. (Thus there are "libertarians" who really amount to plain old-fashioned utopian anarchists, and there are other "libertarians" who make so many concessions to statism that their position is indistinguishable from those in which liberty is demeaned.) The same could be observed about practically any point of view in virtually any area of controversy. The crazy and bland versions simply aren't worth the time in an honest intellectual examination. It seems that it is most advisable to select a reasonably formidable, distinctive, yet not impossible statement of the view one selects for scrutiny, so as not to build into the version obvious seeds of destruction.

Let me explain a few important points about libertarianism. It is, first of all, a political doctrine. It should be distinguished from the "metaphysical libertarianism" related to the problem of the freedom of the will;[16] from "social libertarianism," namely, the view that concerning voluntary human activities and associations everything not involving coercion is equally proper, morally correct, immune from valid moral criticism, rebuke, ostracism, and other forms of opposition and condemnation;[17] from "moral libertarianism" or libertinism, namely, the view that all freely chosen conduct has *equal* merit from the point of view of what is right and wrong in human behavior.[18]

Different arguments have been advanced in support of political libertarianism, but the doctrine itself is a claim as to what is permissible for human beings to do toward each other by means of the aid of force or its threat, nothing more. This claim has been the result of different arguments, some of which are unsound, others invalid, but some indeed theoretically adequate for showing that in human communities force should only be used—in all of its extremely complicated manifestations, possibilities, and threats—for the purpose of protecting and preserving human individual liberty, nothing else.[19] Whether this conclusion can be established, whether it is proper to look to reasoned arguments and theories to establish conclusions bearing on political life, whether any considerations might supersede a conclusion so established (e.g., requiring that although liberty should be furthered politically, something besides politics requires its neglect in certain circumstances)—are relevant issues. But let us be very clear about the principal fact: libertarianism is a claim about the scope of permissible force or threat of force among human beings, including human beings who constitute the governing administration of a given human community; it is a political claim or theory and not some other, however much it may presuppose a variety of other, nonpolitical claims.[20] If one assumes that this claim itself embodies the suppositions of its various arguments, then one prejudices one's criticism against a wide variety of libertarian thought. After all, the same conclusions can be derived from different sets of premises. This is an elementary point of logic. And even if some arguments for liberty are inadequate, it does not follow that none better are available. And indeed the doctrine on which all libertarians are in agreement has been defended on various philosophical grounds.

These and other points need to be kept in mind in order to appreciate what is at stake in the discussion of libertarianism. But there is another point that has especially direct bearing on discussing this political outlook. Unlike most others, libertarian politics, in particular, may not be assimilated to non-political ideas and ideals. It is distinctive precisely in its firm specification concerning the scope of politics in human life, namely, with the point that liberty is the paramount value to be sought by way of politics. The rest of human existence needs to be developed in an atmosphere of freedom, with all the creativity and ingenuity available to human beings. In these areas there may exist firm standards. But experimentation may also be proper. Political principles, stated explicitly, must however guide the most awesome and dangerous instrument of human interaction, namely physical force. Such force is permissible and useful only in repelling force, not in building character, love, faith, scientific knowledge, etc.[21] Libertarianism is not addressed directly to these other spheres of human life because the method of politics cannot be extended to these spheres with moral and practical legitimacy.

What are some arguments for libertarianism? Actually, as far back in recorded intellectual history as Lao Tzu in the East and Alcibiades in the West, certain libertarian ideas are clearly detectable. In Xenophon's *Memorabilia* the young Alcibiades shows Pericles that only that concept of law is valid which precludes the use of force except for retaliatory and defensive purposes.[22] Aristotle discusses the views of the sophist Lycophron who believed that the function of government is to guarantee mutual rights;[23] he also confronts the city planner Hippodamus who thought that only conduct wrong in itself—insult, injury and homicide—should be prohibited.[24] Later on in the West, William of Ockham developed certain ideas about natural rights that stress the requirement for moral choice in every man, thus limiting the range of human interaction.[25] Locke explicitly asserts that each individual is to be regarded as free and independent of the authority of others (in maturity, obviously), and may be subjected to elaborate legal government only with his own consent.[26] Mill thought that liberty should be protected and preserved wherever none has harmed another, mainly so as to secure progress.[27] Spencer advocated natural rights on grounds that human evolution clearly points to a system of such rights as most in conformity with evolutionary progress.[28] Albert Nock did not believe that the moral nature of man could be preserved without his liberty being protected.[29] Ludwig von Mises believed that the economic activities of society could not continue in a most effective and sensible way unless a free market prevails and the price structure is permitted to serve as the means of communication.[30] Ayn Rand thought that the proper end of human life, to be pursued by each individual in accordance with standards of rationality, could not be voluntarily sought by everyone except in a free society based on the rights of man.[31] Robert Nozick holds that the assumption of individual rights within a human community is the best assurance we have that the structure of that community will not violate our moral precepts and intuitions.[32] And there are varieties on the libertarian argument beyond these more or less prominent versions.[33] Virtually all of these thinkers have contributed to the libertarian political tradition, even if, as in the case of Mill, Spencer, and some others, they did not remain libertarians even to the degree to be expected from them in their own times.[34]

Among contemporary representatives of these different strains of libertarianism all agree with the central libertarian ideal, namely, that none should initiate force against another. But a division among libertarians beyond some of the more theoretical issues has bothered many conservatives. This is the split on the issue of government. The anarchist libertarians, led by Professor Murray N. Rothbard, whose libertarianism rests on the two traditions of Lockean natural rights and Austrian economics,[35] hold that governments by definition *initiate* coercion, so they are incompatible with libertarianism. "Limited government" libertarianism, found mainly in the writings of Ayn Rand, John Hospers, and Robert Nozick, conceives government along lines consistent with libertarian principles. It is difficult to comment on the substance of the controversy. It goes on at the present in full force and involves claims and counterclaims of considerable complexity. Moreover, in my view, anarchist libertarians are only seeming anarchists.[36] They use language that appears to condemn a government with exclusive jurisdictional authority within a given community (and in a given area that is homogeneous and makes the enforcement of law therefore possible). What anarchist libertarians deny is that governments have any legitimate authority to exclude alternate contenders in the task of protecting and preserving the rights of individuals. Those libertarians who advocate government claim that while such exclusion appears to be arbitrary and unjustified, and often has been throughout history, there need be nothing arbitrary about it when properly understood.

The appearance of the language of anarchism in libertarian circles has led conservatives with libertarian leanings to become fearful and suspicious. Some even claim that consistent libertarianism leads to anarchism and the denial of anarchism is a minor inconsistency that one must simply accept. (Milton Friedman seems to believe this, in contrast to David, his son, who has argued for anarchist libertarianism, though from a framework different from Rothbard's.)[37] In general, those who find the institution of government important in society, even if cut down to its appropriate proportions, have regarded libertarianism with suspicion because of the anarchist rhetoric, if not substance. Anarchists of the Kropotkin or Bakunin varieties, on the other hand, have made clear that they regard "anarcho-libertarianism" as a fraud, since by their doctrine the institution and protection of private property requires some kind of legal authority, government, or similar institution in society.[38]

Conservatives have always found government important, but have not liked the drift toward totalitarianism evident in contemporary statist trends. They have stressed the inefficiency of most (federal) statist undertakings but have eschewed, I believe, a principled rejection of statism.

Generally stated, conservatives, in the United States, would leave to a federal government the job of military protection even if this might involve conscription, extensive foreign alliances, and foreign intervention. They would leave to state, county, municipal, and even more localized governmental/community bodies concerns such as upholding standards in education, science, art, and entertainment. Moreover, conservatives do not object to a free market. But they would place fewer aspects of human life at the disposal of market transaction and decision than would libertarians. Take the area of the arts or entertainment, for instance, where we may properly classify as corrupt such offerings as pornographic novels and movies, etc. Conservatives would welcome here, let alone permit, a local government's imposition of regulations excluding or restricting the production, sale, and purchase of such items that fit within a definition of pornography (arrived at by the consensus to be used in communities—involving quasi-democratic and quasi-aristocratic methods).[39] Although conservatives would deny that obscenity and pornography are indefinable, as modern liberals have maintained, they would not try to define these by some rationalist argument but would leave the matter to the customs and traditions that have come to prevail in the area where the concerns arise.[40]

The conservative is concerned more with having certain standards of conduct insisted upon, whereas the libertarian is concerned more with avoiding any semblance of imposition, not to mention coercion, in human community life. The more this is all they focus upon, the more the two will find each other in disagreement, indeed in hostile camps. But this is to stress extremes. Credible versions of libertarianism and conservatism in America remain allied on numerous important fronts. To make this evident, I will spell out several rarely observed aspects of libertarianism. Misunderstanding about these cannot but serve to under-cut the goals of both. It is possible that even after all the clarification, important differences will remain. Yet no one need be extremely concerned about this. Even a moderate individualism will call to mind that many of the differences among human beings only appear to be about principles. More often they stem from idiosyncracsies, not unimpor-tant but still personal peculiarities—that is, the irreducible individual differences among human beings that have slipped into abstract theoretical reflections without clear notice.

The area where conservatives appear least to understand libertarianism concerns the issue of moral standards, espe-cially in the area of social ethics. Here no outright coercion is at stake, yet conduct may be evident to the community at large and influences can make themselves felt to sensi-tive individuals or those who are especially vulnerable. In short, it is in the area of social standards that conservatives have the most trouble with libertarianism, apart from the more philosophical matters of rationalism, theism, mod-ernism, etc., even if these are not entirely separate.

What are social issues? For the libertarian the distinction between government, society, and the individual applies here.[41] A government bears on everyone's life in a society and acts *for* everyone. It may thus act only in accordance with principles that apply to all, namely, regard for the individual human rights of each person.[42] In society, however, while all must at least abide by these principles, there are numerous other valid concerns. Different individuals, with different kinds of backgrounds, professional aims, temperaments, talents, and so forth, will develop a great variety of social relations. Are there standards which would warrant either promoting or discouraging and undermining certain kinds of social relations? Might one not insist even on their being prescribed or made illegal, respectively?

For instance, while one might not endorse prohibition, it may perhaps be claimed that prostitution, sexual frivolity, sacrilege, abuse of parental authority, or drunken binges, are not socially desirable. It might not be justified to advocate laws against these practices. But might not one maintain that, e.g., all else being equal, homosexuality is less healthy and admirable a form of sexuality than heterosexuality? Could not one maintain that when it comes to artistic exhibitions, the presentation of a festival of "porno flicks" should far from merit the same respect as a festival of the plays of Shakespeare? One might even go further and vociferously condemn divorce, pre-marital sexual relations, and avant-garde literature, all as a matter of standards and taste.

Is it possible for libertarians to do this? Mustn't they be silent on these in the light of restricting themselves to matters of politics, which to them means only the defending of human liberty? Surely such a merely negative approach is inadequate for these purposes. If this follows from libertarianism, is it not then in fact deficient for coming to terms with human community life? Would not all those activities one should regard as wrong, debasing, degrading, vile, vicious, and so forth, barring those that involve outright coercion, have to be regarded by libertarians as perfectly acceptable? Would not silence about the quality of such social matters imply official approval? Would it not follow that if there is permission, from the point of view of the law, to produce, sell, and purchase pornography, the law would in fact be promoting the same? Does it not follow that in giving official protection to the purveyors of bad social practices in the name of individual liberty—e.g., when a federal court gives the first amendment as grounds for prohibiting a town mayor from closing the doors of a movie house that is showing pornography— one is clearly endorsing conduct that is socially improper and is at once undermining the currency of liberty?

These and many other questions, put in more or less fair and intellectually honest ways, have been posed to libertarianism by conservative writers. Not every libertarian would be able to answer these questions (and their logical kin) to the satisfaction of many conservatives. Because, however, many who write on the topic have either omitted researching whether libertarians have answered these questions satisfactorily or have simply picked on select and very narrow libertarian texts to show that libertarians are not up to the task, an attempt to answer these questions here will be of some use.[43] The answers I can give will be reflective enough of at least a prominent line of libertarian theory so that they can safely be regarded as "libertarian answers."

Libertarian political theory implies that a government

functions properly when it upholds justice in human relations by the standard of natural human rights—as initially developed in John Locke's *Second Treatise* and given more depth and scope by contemporary libertarians.[44] Such a government would fulfill both the ancient and the modern role of state, namely, the encouragement of virtue and the promotion of peace and prosperity. The former would be achieved by securing liberty for all, which is a necessary condition for the virtuous life in society.[45] If one acts because of coercion or its threat, one cannot make moral choices. A legal system in which freedom is not protected and preserved prevents individual moral responsibility. So government that protects and preserves human freedom encourages individual moral responsibility and human virtue. Such a government also makes possible the development of peaceful means by which to achieve various personal and social goals. One of these social goals is the promotion of improved conditions of life. And while in libertarian theory no one has a natural *right* to have welfare or prosperity provided by others, it is implicit within the theory that advancement in the arts, sciences, education, leisure, material wealth, and psychological health—are all valuable elements in human life, even if not in equal measure to all.

Libertarian political theory holds it as a violation of the nature of man to engage in coercive dictation of other people's social practices, sexual habits, religious affiliations, and so forth. Nevertheless libertarianism does not preclude other means for advancing social goals. Some of these are close voluntary substitutes for outright coercion. Moreover, parental responsibility in a free society (along libertarian lines) would not preclude the use of physical force against a child within the dictates of reason. A child is normally incapable of making rational decisions concerning its behavior and could, unless at times forcibly yet reasonably forbidden from doing so, place itself in severe danger. This form of coercion is not excluded in libertarian theory.

Coercion among normal adults is forbidden, with exceptions allowed only if they have been properly defended in a court of law guided by rational rules of evidence and libertarian principle (incorporated in the common and constitutional law).[46] Voluntary approaches to social direction, in the variety of ways we refer to as ostracism, rebuke, boycott, etc., are available for use to everyone and anyone. These ways can be developed into massive and severe instruments of social control and change. It would be quite illegitimate to dismiss these methods as ineffectual, especially in light of the entirely ineffectual character of coercive efforts to promote or stifle personal and social development. The libertarians cannot and will not give the false promise that coercion will guarantee the rooting out of evil and the promotion of good. The libertarian is prepared, however, to spell out realistic noncoercive prospects of achieving these ends. Outside the government's proper peace-keeping and retaliatory functions, there is ample room for the libertarian to introduce non-political means so as to cope with the problems and challenges of personal and social life.

Let me stress this again. Libertarianism is a political theory, an answer to the natural and central political question: In accordance with what basic principle(s) should a human community be organized? Never mind now that such a (rationalist) approach *appears* to assume that one can simply create society. Libertarians realize well enough that social systems emerge and evolve. But they also realize that a crucial factor in this evolution is precisely how this question is answered by human beings. So, the libertarian is interested, *as* libertarian, in offering for serious consideration his basic principle as the content of a community's legal system or constitution. Contrary to what critics of the free society have said, be they Marxists such as Marcuse and Fromm or conservatives like Burke and Kristol, the principles of liberty do not preclude a broader ethical framework. These principles of liberty are, as it were, the political tip of a very large iceberg which represents a general philosophy of existence and human life. True, in a complete philosophical system politics is not independent from other elements. But it *is* distinguishable, so that political ideas may in turn be supported in isolation from their underpinnings.

The broader ethical framework that gives backing to libertarian political principles has not been fully attended to in the past by prominent classical liberals and libertarians, mainly because ethics itself has always been viewed as giving license for coercion.[47] If you know what Johnny should do, you may coerce him, even if it isn't little Johnny but mature John whom we are considering now! Marxists have certainly tried to convince us that if we know what is objectively socially useful, we may establish a state and make everyone's conduct conform to this. In an intellectual atmosphere in which this association between virtue (or principles of morality) and coercion prevails, it is no surprise that advocates of liberty remain silent about virtue.[48] Whether it be satisfaction of the will of God, the provision of some secular (hypothetical) social contract, the utilitarian provision for the greatest happiness of the greatest number, or the ushering in of the culmination of the historical dialectical progress, in each case such value theories have allowed for, even required, coercing people to achieve the value in question.

It is a widely held view about values that only if they are intrinsic—as it were, present *within* what is to be valued—are they objective. This tends to support the view that an individual's *choice* of the behavior that is worthy is not central to the merits of this behavior, so that the liberty of the acting individual is thus regarded as negligible.[49] This has at times fostered the dichotomization of human virtue (i.e., the human good) and individual liberty (i.e., the choice to act virtuously).

It is not then surprising that those who have, perhaps only through commonsense reflection, perceived the importance of liberty—e.g., economists, who are always being criticized for not giving enough heed to morality[50]—would not eagerly embrace the moral point of view and indeed proclaim their own concerns or discipline value-free. Under the perspective that the value which some state of affairs or end or behavior embodies is the goal to be achieved—not our own moral excellence, which only we as individuals can achieve—the understanding has emerged that people may be forced to do what needs to be done to achieve the good. It is the state of having *reached* the end that is morally relevant, not the process of having lived *by seeking it* or some other self-perfecting approach. This view has been devastating in the modern age.

So one main reason conservatives distrust libertarianism is that they have focused on the political results of a comprehensive philosophical outlook that has libertarianism as its political theory, namely, the view that liberty should be protected and preserved. But there is much more to this outlook. Libertarianism is but a small, politically relevant portion of it, unlike classical liberalism that preceded it.[51]

The broader framework underlying libertarianism is in the tradition of Aristotelian philosophy. This is the best broader framework; not, however, the only one offered. (I assume that we are concerned with a formidable defense, not with incomplete, sloganized versions.)[52] The main Aristotelian ingredient is metaphysical pluralism, which means roughly that reality does not have to be, nor is as we can clearly perceive, one kind of thing, but has the potential for manifesting itself in numerous ways. There is a monism, too, in this metaphysics, namely, that certain basic principles govern the *whole* of reality including all distinctive realms and features of it.[53] Along lines of such a basic view, the emergence of value considerations can make sense. Ethics, politics, aesthetics, and so forth are all intelligible without having to introduce something perplexing and untenable, namely, supernaturalism.[54]

When life emerges in reality, objective values emerge too. The living have a lot to lose by dying. And in the case of human life, value considerations take on a *moral* component because individual human beings are *responsible* to identify the values that will sustain and improve their lives—that is, because of the phenomenon of free will.

Since we are responsible—like it or not—for living well or badly, we must eschew any substitute for this responsibility lest we shed our very humanity in the process. Thus political liberty. The philosophy that underlies the robust theory of libertarian politics can be seen, thus, to secure a natural—as distinct from a supernatural—place for objective personal, social, and political norms. And this is just one feature of libertarianism that conservative critics have denied.[55] They have focused on the fact that many arguments for liberty—going as far back as Taoism and as close to our time as the position of Professor Milton Friedman—have been based on moral skepticism.[56] Yet there have also been other arguments, which critics have not discussed in detail and are still discussing only when the famous among us make them, even if only incompletely.[57]

It would not be surprising, however, that arguments for what to many appears as a very good idea are usually incomplete. The identification of principles in any domain of reality is gradual, rocky, evolving. Man is not omniscient and man often makes tragic detours as he seeks the truth. This is ever more so when we reach realms involving norms, the difference between right and wrong, good and evil. In normative areas there is often great resistance to the process of careful, objective study. One should expect this from those who would be identified as failures were the truth known even incompletely, and sometimes from those with good will, but eager to caution us about dogmatism and, in politics, about authoritarianism or the temptation many human beings have to claim a monopoly on the truths of ethics and politics.

Today the libertarian political principle does, however,

enjoy the support of a reasonably well developed, rational philosophy. It may, with some risks stemming from necessary brevity, be summarized as follows: Once an individual chooses to live, that individual has committed himself to living well or properly, namely in accordance with his nature; libertarianism is the political theory which best takes into account man's nature, namely, his essence as a free, rational living being whose conduct can only be made morally worthwhile by the individual himself by sustaining his commitment. This kind of life, with all of the diversity *and* universality it entails—based on the broad human and highly specialized individual and other characteristics every individual possesses—is what should be chosen by each individual. This kind of life involves an array of human virtues (honesty, productivity, prudence, courage, fortitude, justice, self-respect, etc.), but these virtues must be sustained and practiced by choice and their precise interpretation must be adjusted to the individual's own case. For our purposes it is crucial to note that this kind of life is *not owed* to anyone; so it entails no other obligations than those freely chosen by the individual, even if it is true that once chosen these obligations should be fulfilled, and even if it is true that some of these obligations should be chosen by an individual because of his humanity and individual identity. And all of this is to take place in the world we are familiar with, involving numerous implications bearing on various aspects of reality (e.g., parenthood, friendship, career plans, political concerns, ownership, professional tasks, and so forth). So as to achieve such feats as a matter of individual responsibility, it is necessary that everyone enjoy the freedom in society that human beings can insure for each other without in any way being required to become indentured to others. Therefore, the free society, via the respect of everyone's naturally derived rights to life, liberty and property, is the best political order for every human being.

Concerning the social elements of a mature libertarian political theory—numerous implications may be identified. Those, however, are very specialized because of the volatile nature of human circumstances. Nevertheless, a few claims that have been made as to the social philosophy of libertarianism need attention.

For example, some maintain that libertarianism presupposes a hedonistic ethic. This is not true—it presupposes an eudaimonistic individualism, as can be discerned from what has already been said here.[58] Is libertinism implicit in the advocacy of liberty as the highest political principle? No—libertarianism only prohibits the *forcible* squelching of indecent conduct, not its vigorous criticism, opposition, boycott or denunciation in peaceful ways. A preoccupation with material wealth is supposed to be implicit in libertarianism. But there is no requirement in that political doctrine to the effect that human beings ought to strive for material wealth, even if ordinary prudence would be expected from anyone as regards his material needs and wants. Nor is libertarianism anti-religious. Nothing in the doctrine requires the forfeiting of religious worship, although, it is true, the argument underlying libertarian politics stresses the rational identification of reality, thus by implication, fundamental reliance on faith for purposes of understanding ethics and politics is eschewed. And libertarianism is often said to presuppose a mechanistic materialistic conception of human nature. This is equally misguided. The pluralistic metaphysics that forms the basis of the philosophy in support of libertarian politics does not prejudge in favor of mechanistic materialism, even if some economic libertarians lead one to believe this by virtue of their particular social science methodology.[59]

No doubt, even a robust philosophical case for libertarianism, as outlined here, will conflict with several of the main tenets of contemporary conservative thought. For example, a rather optimistic view underlies the libertarian doctrine, in contrast to the view some leading conservatives have advocated. But this optimism is by no means committed to the doctrine that man is naturally or automatically good, but only to the view that man *can* be good by his own sustained effort. When conservatives claim that man has a "proclivity toward violence and sin,"[60] the libertarian would have to object. Neither argument nor historical evidence supports this claim. Only a very selective, sensationalist or journalistic view of human history omits from consideration the considerable degree of human virtue and good that permeates human existence—if mainly away from the limelight. But the libertarian rejects the modern liberal, secular utopian view of man's perfectibility (by the rational organization of society or the dialectics of history). Man is perfectible, but only by his own sustained disciplined effort. And if this be optimism, the libertarian will have to plead guilty. What the libertarian is concerned with *qua* libertarian is to make possible—not to falsely guarantee— for each human being to aspire to goodness in his own circumstances, admitting that this aspiration may be neglected. And this is not utopianism.

There is another, less fundamental but quite emotion-packed issue on which libertarians and conservatives are frequently in serious disagreement, namely, foreign policy. The foreign policy of a free society, as its domestic policy, stresses the social primacy of liberty. This amounts to a strict foreign policy of *defensivism*, as explained in an essay by Professor Eric Mack.[61] Some libertarians insist on an isolationist foreign policy, but that cannot be derived from the libertarian political framework, contrary to their contentions.[62] As to the implications of libertarian defensivist foreign policy for the conduct of the present American government, this is a very complicated matter, but not unmanageable. Libertarians have not developed the specialization for purposes of answering the numerous particular policy questions the present American government faces, but they are, quite justifiably, very suspicious of the wisdom of the *status quo*. In my view the few libertarians who have made contributions to this area of concern have remained far too abstract and have succeeded mainly in raising questions, not in answering them.[63] Still, it is not an exaggeration to maintain that conservatives would find libertarians too complacent about the threat of international communism, just as libertarians find conservatives too complacent about the threat of domestic authoritarianism in the wake of a policy of virtual Wilsonian imperialism. The point that should be admitted is that some very serious thinking needs to be done to discover—instead of dogmatically to assert—what a free society's foreign policy implies for those who are seeking to establish such a society from within a mixed society such as America is today.

To conclude, let me recall here some thoughts expressed by an individual whom some conservatives have called upon to give support to their anti-libertarian concerns.[64] The late Leo Strauss made numerous relevant points regarding the issues surrounding the present discussion, but three are especially germane. First, Strauss identified the good life for man as:

> simply the life in which the requirements of man's natural inclinations are fulfilled in the proper order to the highest possible degree, the life of a man who is awake to the highest possible degree, the life of a man in whose soul nothing lies waste.[65]

He also believed that: "political freedom and especially that political freedom that justifies itself by the pursuit of human excellence...requires the highest degree of vigilance."[66]

And finally he held: "There is no adequate solution to the problem of virtue or happiness on the political or social plane."[67]

If we put these three ideas together—which, it seems to me, do give expression to Strauss' own views (as rare as this is in his writing)—we will arrive at the libertarianism I have been speaking of throughout this discussion. This libertarianism is, put plainly, the view that the task of politics is liberty,[68] nothing more or less, and the task of virtue, human excellence or happiness, is a task that only the individual on his own can strive to fulfill either alone or in personal and voluntary association with others, never by force or coercion.[69]

Notes

1. E.g., John Hospers, *Libertarianism* (Los Angeles: Nash Publishing, 1971), Tibor R. Machan, *Human Rights and Human Liberties* (Chicago: Nelson-Hall, 1975), Robert Nozick, *Anarchy, State, and Utopia* (New York: Basic Books, 1974), Ayn Rand, *Capitalism, The Unknown Ideal* (New York: Signet Books, 1967), Murray N. Rothbard, *Power and Market* (Menlo Park, California: Institute for Humane Studies, 1971). Rand denied that she was a libertarian; yet her political principles were those of libertarianism and her work is frequently cited in libertarian literature as providing a basis for libertarianism.

2. E.g., CATO Institute, Washington, D.C.; Institute for Humane Studies, Fairfax, Virginia; Center for Libertarian Studies, New York, New York; The Reason Foundation, Santa Barbara, California. None of these organizations is in political affiliation with the Libertarian Party and they are all educational, non-profit outfits.

3. Some of the subjects of serious dispute include whether government is consistent with libertarianism, whether libertarian principles give support to the claim that abortion should not be illegal, whether isolationism or some other form of principled foreign policy—e.g., defensivism, as explained by Eric Mack, "Permissible Defense," *Reason* 8 (July 1977): 26-31—is proper from a libertarian point of view. On abortion, see *Reason* 9 (April 1978).

4. The list is very long indeed. Examples may be found in the pages of *Commentary, National Review, The New Republic,* and *The Nation,* as far as general readership magazines are concerned. Scholarly criticisms, especially of Robert Nozick's libertarian arguments, have appeared in *Philosophy and Public Affairs, The Public Interest, Political Theory, Canadian Journal of Philosophy, Modern Age, The Intercollegiate Review, Journal of Philosophy, Ethics, Human Rights,* and many other publications.

5. See note 3. Among major publishers who have issued works on libertarian thought are Basic Books, Macmillan Publishing Company, University of Chicago Press, Open Court, and Prentice-Hall.

6. For example, at Harvard University, University of California at Berkeley, Stanford University, Princeton University, University of Southern California, and many other prominent universities libertarianism is covered in

philosophy, economics, and political science courses regularly.

7. No other political doctrine emphasized the concept of human rights as libertarianism. But libertarians have popularized the idea of victimless crimes, decriminalization, tax resistance, deregulation, and restitution for victims of crimes. The language of academic political theory has adopted many of the ideas found in Robert Nozick's work, although it is doubtful that this indicates any substantive decline in the leftist orientation of academic humanists. Here Nozick's own prominence and philosophical competence accounts for the development of libertarian flavored discussions.

8. We may recall here the Jaffa/Kendall and Jaffa/Bradford debates in conservative intellectual circles.

9. Any attention to libertarian and conservative publications will reveal just how often such writers as Yale Brozen, Henry Hazlitt, Milton Friedman, William Rickenbacker, and William Niskanen have appeared in both of their pages, usually expressing concerns with the topics mentioned.

10. E.g., Russell Kirk, *The Conservative Mind from Burke to Eliot* (Chicago: Henry Regnery, 1953), Arianna Stassinopoulos, *After Reason* (New York: Stein and Day, 1978), and M. E. Bradford, "A Better Guide than Reason: The Politics of John Dickinson," *Modern Age* 21 (Winter 1977): 39-49. In most conservative criticisms of reason it is Cartesian or mechanistic rationality that is at issue. Moreover, not only conservatives but many others consider this version of rationality inadequate. See, e.g., Paul Feyerabend, *Against Method* (London: NLB, 1975) and F. A. Hayek, *Law, Legislation, and Liberty* (Chicago: University of Chicago Press, 1973), vol. 1. For a most formidable criticism of the form of rationalism at issue here, see Michael Oakeshott, *Rationalism in Politics* (New York: Basic Books, 1962), although it would be very risky to categorize Oakeshott's position here.

11. For a prominent thinker who has often been considered more of a libertarian than a conservative, though welcome in both intellectual traditions, F. A. Hayek, *op. cit.*, appears to join conservatives and Michael Oakeshott in being suspicious of reason but only in the constructivist sense. Other libertarians cannot be aligned in this respect with great precision, but many with an ethical argument for the free society would regard themselves as Aristotelians or Thomists, while those with an empirical bent may be regarded as very respectful toward Humean or positivistic empiricism. For more on this, see my *Human Rights and*

Human Liberties, 258-64, *passim*.

12. But, note that their conception of reason is significantly different from what most conservatives consider narrow.

13. E.g., libertarians oppose any law, *qua* legally enforceable measure in human community life, that prescribes personal or social moral principles or rules—including those that are valid and true—and that prohibits their violation. Thus it may be wrong to engage in premarital sexual intercourse but when done with full consent, it may not be prohibited; and though it may be morally right to publish books with taste and moral awareness, a publisher may not be forced to do so (or punished for not having done so). The complications of a nation with massive public facilities—run at taxpayers' expense and given state direction—cannot be discussed here, although libertarians are far from unaware of them in their various writings. See, e.g., the 37 essays in Tibor R. Machan, ed., *The Libertarian Alternative* (Chicago: Nelson-Hall, 1974).

14. The evidence may be found in the widespread support such regulatory proposals have received in various elections from conservative voters and political representatives.

15. Bearing directly on politics, the rejection of the rationalist approach often results in the rejection of the so-called absolutist versions of the principles of the free society. See, e.g., Walter Berns, *The First Amendment and the Future of American Democracy* (New York: Basic Books, 1976).

16. E.g., C.D. Broad, "Determinism, Indeterminism, and Libertarianism," in *Ethics and the History of Philosophy* (London: Routledge & Kegan Paul, 1952).

17. See note 13.

18. Many conservatives believe that the secular bent in libertarian theories necessarily presupposes the subjectivist ethics of libertinism. Also, they object to the humanism often implicit within libertarianism. See, e.g., David Ehrenfeld, *The Arrogance of Humanism* (New York: Oxford University Press, 1978). The classic rejection of Locke's libertarianism may be found to be based on the alleged egoism of Locke. See, e.g., Leo Strauss, *Natural Right and History* (Chicago: University of Chicago Press, 1953). Strauss, unlike most conservatives, is more critical of the narrow Hobbesian egoism than of egoism *per se*. For a type of ethical theory that stresses the importance of the individual and would serve well as the moral underpinnings of libertarianism, see David L. Norton, *Personal Destinies, A Philosophy of Ethical Individualism* (Princeton: Princeton University

Press, 1976). See also my "Recent Work in Ethical Egoism," *American Philosophical Quarterly* 16 (January 1979): 1-15, and "Review of *Personal Destinies*," *American Journal of Jurisprudence* (1979): 213-26.

19. For a discussion of what counts as an adequate theory in this and other realms of inquiry, see my "Rational Choice and Public Affairs," *Theory and Decision* 12 (September 1980): 229-58. Since no man can reasonably aspire to produce a final, unchangeable understanding of a reality that is dynamic and by no means finished, only open-ended theories can be considered even plausible, let alone adequate, especially in the human sciences. But certain criteria do apply which require a theory to be consistent and fair to the facts.

20. One might consider that the theory of evolution is a biological theory, even though its validity presupposes numerous facts in chemistry, physics, epistemology, etc. The fact that Darwin did not address all the issues in these fields with bearing on his own sphere of concern does not deter from the truth of his views.

21. Force, even in its petty versions—e.g., government regulation (which former President Ford called "petty tyrannies")—is the enemy of creativity, imagination, flourishing. An active being's primary faculty, namely, his reason, and all of what relies on it, are undercut when force is interjected. This is why slavery, massive or minute, simply cannot work as well as liberty, as the Nazi and Soviet experiments (!) demonstrated.

22. *The Way of Lao Tzu* (Indianapolis, Indiana: Bobbs-Merrill, 1963).

23. Aristotle, *Politics* III.9: 1280b10.

24. *Ibid.*, III.7: 1267b38.

25. William of Ockham, *Opus Nonaginta Dierum*, Chapter 65.

26. John Locke, *Second Treatise on Civil Government*, ed. J. Gough (Oxford: Oxford University Press, 1956).

27. John Stuart Mill, *On Liberty*, ed. C.V. Shields (Indianapolis, Indiana: Bobbs-Merrill, 1957), 66. The progressivist character of Mill's thought is explained in Gertrude Himmelfarb, *On Liberty and Liberalism* (New York: Knopf, 1974).

28. Herbert Spencer, *The Principles of Ethics* (Indianapolis: Liberty Classics, 1978).

29. Albert Jay Nock, *Our Enemy, the State* (Caldwell, Idaho: Caxton Printers, 1946).

30. Ludwig von Mises, *Socialism* (London: Jonathan Cape, 1936).

31. Ayn Rand, "The Objectivist Ethics," in *The Virtue of Selfishness, A New*

Concept of Egoism (New York: Signet, 1964).

32. Nozick, *op. cit.*

33. For the individualist anarchism that has been stressed by some as an essential part of the libertarian tradition, see James J. Martin, *Men Against the State* (Colorado Springs: Ralph Myles, 1970) and Murray N. Rothbard's *For a New Liberty* (New York: Macmillan, 1973) and *Power and Market*, *op. cit.*, which present a compilation of Lockean and Austrian economic arguments for anarchist libertarianism.

34. By this remark I aim to stress that there is nothing odd about regarding someone as part of a tradition even if that individual's views are not exactly expressed in contemporary terminology.

35. See note 33.

36. See my *Human Rights and Human Liberties*, 143-60. In my work I discuss several versions of anarchism, including the views of Professor Rothbard. To date, however, discussions of Rothbard's position have centered on Nozick's arguments against anarchist libertarianism. See the essays in *The Journal of Libertarian Studies* 1 (Winter 1977). None of these discussions comes to terms with the arguments I offer against anarchist libertarianism.

37. David Friedman, *The Machinery of Freedom* (New York: Harper and Row, 1973). For Milton Friedman's explicit view on this issue, see Joe Cobb, Tibor Machan, and Ralph Raico, "an Interview with Milton Friedman," *Reason* 6 (December 1974).

38. See several letters to the editor of *Penthouse* magazine, March 1974, in response to an essay about Professor Rothbard by Samuel Blumenfeld in *Penthouse*, November 1973. See also Sam Wells, "Anarcho-Capitalism is Not Anarchism, and Political Competition is Not Economic Competition," *Frontlines* 1 (January 1979).

39. E.g., see Irving Kristol, "Pornography, Obscenity, and the Case for Censorship," in J. Feinberg and H. Gross, eds., *Philosophy of Law* (Belmont, California: Dickenson, 1975), and Walter Berns, "Free Speech and Free Government," *The Political Science Reviewer* 2 (1972): 217-41. In this as in other of his writings, Berns insists on associating libertarianism with the doctrine that truth is relative; yet no such doctrine underlies libertarianism; quite the contrary, considering that libertarians insist on the universality of the truth of the principle of liberty. (Nor, as Berns insists, do libertarians embrace the legal philosophy of Oliver W. Holmes, Jr., who was a pragmatist and completely eschewed the doctrine of natural law, one of

the most often cited theories in support of libertarianism.)

40. Gary North, "Pornography, Community, Law," *National Review* 25 (August 31, 1973).

41. On a microcosmic level this distinction would be reflected in, e.g., referee, game, and player, in basketball, with only the first having a claim to authority for using force. See Albert J. Nock, *op. cit.*

42. This is explained further in my *Human Rights and Human Liberties*, chapter 4.

43. For some rather clear examples of offhand references to libertarianism, see Stephen J. Tonsor, "Liberty and Equality as Absolutes," *Modern Age* 23 (Winter 1979): 8; John P. East, "Leo Strauss and American Conservatism," *Modern Age* 21 (Winter 1977): 18. See, especially, Ernest van den Haag, "Libertarians and Conservatives," *National Review* (June 8, 1979).

44. It is Leo Strauss and his students who teach the view that Locke's work is not actually *bona fide* political philosophy. See Michael P. Zuckert, "The Recent Literature on Locke's Political Philosophy," *The Political Science Reviewer* 5 (1975): 271-304.

45. For more on this, see my *Human Rights and Human Liberties*, 137, and "Some Consideration of the Common Good," *Journal of Human Relations* 18, no. 3 (1970): 979-94. See also Frank S. Meyer, *In Defense of Freedom* (Chicago: Henry Regnery, 1962), Donald J. Devine, *Does Freedom Work?* (Ottawa, Illinois: Caroline House Books, 1978), and, especially, Douglas Den Uyl, "Freedom and Virtue," *Reason Papers* 5 (1979): 1-12. A somewhat similar view is defended in Alan Gewirth, *Reason and Morality* (Chicago: University of Chicago Press, 1978), although Gewirth believes that capability, too, is a necessary condition of morality and therefore one has a right to welfare (i.e., the provision of such capabilities by others). For some objections to this and a discussion of a variety of human rights theories, see my "Some Recent Work in Human Rights Theory," *American Philosophical Quarterly* 19 (January 1982): 61-72.

46. A specifically libertarian theory of law has obviously not been developed to the extent other theories have, although the works of F.A. Hayek, Bruno Leoni, Richard Epstein, John Hospers, J. Roger Lee, Randy Barnett, and others offer many insights as to the foreseeable elements of a distinctively libertarian legal code. Since the American political and legal traditions are very close to some crucial aspects of libertarianism, legal theory in America would be of much help in the development of a libertarian legal system.

47. A very good example of this is found in Lord Devlin, *The Enforcement*

of Morals (Oxford: Oxford University Press, 1959). In earlier times, with the close relationship of state and church, the moral commandments were often tantamount to legal edicts. For an argument for liberty which accepts that if one knows that another is doing wrong (or not doing right), one should interfere, see Cobb, Machan, and Raico, "Interview with Milton Friedman," *op. cit.*

48. The Founding Fathers' greater concern for liberty rather than virtue may be appreciated along the present line of analysis.

49. No one quite announces the matter this way, but various doctrines of what *true* liberty means, namely the freedom from hardship, from hunger, from physical or spiritual suffering (even if it does not mean the freedom from the interferences of other human beings) amount precisely to this view.

50. Irving Kristol, "'When Virtue Loses All Her Loveliness'—Some Reflections on Capitalism and the 'Free Society,'" in *Two Cheers for Capitalism* (New York: Basic Books, 1978).

51. Classical liberalism may properly be regarded as far more than a political theory such as libertarianism, since it is philosophically broader, involving ideas about the nature of man, God, value, science, etc. Although libertarianism may indeed be defensible from a very specific philosophical perspective, it is not itself that perspective.

52. Unfortunately critics of libertarianism focus only on the slogans, or those renditions that emanate from very prominent circles, regardless of how complete and comprehensive these may be. See my "Considerations of the Libertarian Alternative," *Harvard Journal of Law and Public Policy* 2 (1979): 103-24, where I examine critical discussions of Nozick's work and try to provide some of the theoretical replies to Nozick's critics based on a libertarian view that is much broader than his.

53. For more on this, see my "Reason, Morality, and the Free Society," in R.L. Cunningham, ed., *Law and Liberty: Essays on F.A. Hayek* (College Station, Texas: Texas A & M University Press, 1979).

54. Moreover, the political theory that presupposes supernaturalism is theoretically flawed by begging one crucial question of political life, namely, by what principles should a human community be governed? To answer that it is to be discovered by revelation, the people who do not experience it will be left automatically in the position of having to accept the words of those who do. The naturalist approach, which relied on man's essential (natural) capacity to reason, begins political inquiry in such a way as to

make it possible for everyone to learn the answers.

55. See note 39, Berns, "Free Speech and Free Government," 237. The argument runs as follows: Prominent thinkers who have advocated what are political theories in the libertarian tradition have asserted the relativity of truth, but truth is not relative even by the implications of their own theory, therefore, libertarianism is false. But this argument is fallacious. It assumes that if "P implies R" is true, but "P" is false, then "R" is false. Yet it has been argued, I believe successfully, that "S implies R," and "S" is true, therefore "R" is proven. We may regard "P" as the view that truth is relative and "R" as the libertarian political theory, while "S" is the view that man has a moral nature so he must choose his own moral excellence. Assuming that both "P" and "S" imply "R", it won't do to keep refuting "P" in order to refute "R".

56. For Friedman's view, see Cobb, Machan, and Raico, "Interview with Milton Friedman," *op. cit.*

57. I am referring to the extraordinarily widespread discussions of Nozick's work, in contrast to the much more comprehensive works of Ayn Rand and Eric Mack. For Mack's work, see his "How to Derive Ethical Egoism," *The Personalist* 52 (Winter 1971): 735-43, "Egoism and Rights," *The Personalist* 54 (Spring 1973): 5-33, and "Egoism and Rights Revisited," *The Personalist* 58 (Summer 1977): 282-88. See also essays by Eric Mack, John Hospers, John O. Nelson, James Sadowsky, Nathaniel Branden, and me in Tibor R. Machan, ed., *The Libertarian Alternative.*

58. See David L. Norton, *Personal Destinies*, for a detailed exposition of this ethical position. I should not leave the impression, however, that Norton is a libertarian. I simply contend that his eudaimonistic individualism provides a correct foundation to libertarian political theory.

59. I have in mind scholars associated with the University of Chicago department of economics, noted for their strict reliance on positivist or empiricist methodology and its presuppositions.

60. Russell Kirk, *The Conservative Mind.*

61. Mack, "Permissible Defense," *op. cit.*

62. R.A. Childs, Jr., editor of *Libertarian Review*, has advocated what he calls "noninterventionism" in American foreign policy, *Libertarian Review* 8 (January 1979): 25, but there is no reason at all to accept that libertarianism implies this. Defensive military action can easily require foreign intervention, even in the affairs of countries that are not the direct enemies of a free society (e.g., when such countries are unjustifiably

complacent about military threats against them *and* such threats, expressed in identifiable actions of course, are also threats against one's own free country).

63. See, e.g., Murray N. Rothbard, "Soviet Foreign Policy: A Revisionist Perspective," *Libertarian Review* 7 (April 1978): 7-23.

64. East, "Leo Strauss," *op. cit.*

65. Leo Strauss, *Natural Right and History*, 2nd edition (Chicago: University of Chicago Press, 1970), 127.

66. *Ibid.*, 131.

67. Strauss, "Restatement on Xenophon's *Hiero*," in *On Tyranny* (Ithaca, New York: Cornell University Press, 1968), 194.

68. This theme is eloquently articulated in Robert F. Sasseen, "Freedom as an End of Politics," *Interpretation* 2 (1971): 105-25.

69. I wish to thank Manuel S. Kalusner, Robert W. Poole, Jr., and the late Dr. David S. Collier for helpful comments on an earlier draft of this essay. Of course, I take full responsibility for my use or misuse of their very generous assistance. I also wish to thank the Earhart and the Reason foundations for making possible my work on this and several related papers.

Frank S. Meyer: The Fusionist as Libertarian Manqué

Murray N. Rothbard

Until a decade or two ago, the conservative spectrum could be comfortably sundered into the "traditionalists" at one pole, the "libertarians" at the other, and the "fusionists" as either judicious synthesizers or muddled moderates (depending on one's point of view) in between. The traditionalists were, I contend, in favor of state-coerced morality; the libertarians were allegedly in favor of liberty but soft on virtue; the fusionists—at least from their own perspective—combined the best of both poles by favoring tradition and morality on the one hand, but freedom of choice and individual rights on the other.

Now, however, it is impossible to sustain these neat classifications. In the first place, the varieties of conservative thought and policy have greatly expanded and diversified in recent years, so that the familiar triad can scarcely suffice any longer. It is difficult to figure out, for example, what the ideologies of the Rev. Jerry Falwell, Frank S. Meyer, M.E. Bradford, Harry Jaffa, Donald Atwell Zoll,

Russell Kirk, Seymour Martin Lipset, and Jude Wanniski have in common; the venerable triad is scarcely enough to encompass them all. Secondly, the libertarians have broken off to form their own movement, and the characterization of them as devoid of concern for morality is distorted and oversimplified, to say the least.

Furthermore, the fusionists used to maintain that, while their success was far from assured among conservative intellectuals, at least the conservative masses were fusionists to the core. But the burgeoning of the Moral Majority and allied movements have at least called this into question.

I propose in this essay to examine conservatism by using as a fulcrum an analysis of the views of the leading conservative fusionist, the late Frank S. Meyer.

The conceptual chaos of conservatism may be traced back to its origins: a reaction against the New Deal. Since modern conservatism emerged in response to the particular leap into statism of the 1930s and 1940s, it necessarily took on the features of any "popular front": that is, defined more by what it opposed than what it stood for. As a result, conservatism came to include a congeries of opponents of the New Deal, who had little positive in common. If we wish to inquire what all of these groups had in common, beyond sheer hatred of Franklin Roosevelt's New Deal, I can think of only one theme linking them all: opposition to egalitarianism, to compulsory levelling by use of state power; beyond that, conservatism is Chaos and Old Night. Even negative reaction to the New Deal no longer suffices for anything like a coherent stance, since not only is there a problem of *which* aspects of the New Deal to focus on, but also whether the post-New Deal system should remain in place and be subject only to marginal adjustment—that is, whether conservatism should be a holding operation—or whether the system should be replaced *in toto.*

At the heart of the dispute between the traditionalists and the libertarians is the question of freedom and virtue: Should virtuous action (however we define it) be compelled, or should it be left up to the free and voluntary choice of the individual? Here only two answers are possible; any fusionist attempt to find a Third Way, a synthesis of the two, would simply be impossible and violate the law of the excluded middle.

In fact, Frank Meyer was, on this crucial issue, squarely in the libertarian camp. In my view, his most important contribution to conservatism was his emphasis that to be virtuous in any meaningful sense, a man's action must be free. It is not simply that freedom and virtue are both important, and that one hopes that freedom of choice will lead to virtuous actions. The point is more forceful: no action *can be* virtuous unless it is freely chosen.

Suppose, for a moment, that we define a virtuous act as bowing in the direction of Mecca every day at sunset. We attempt to persuade everyone to perform this act. But suppose that instead of relying on voluntary conviction we employ a vast number of police to break into everyone's home and see to it that every day they are pushed down to the floor in the direction of Mecca. No doubt by taking such measures we will increase the number of people bowing toward Mecca. But by forcing them to do so, we are taking them out of the realm of action and into mere motion, and we are depriving all these coerced persons of the very possibility of acting morally. By attempting to compel virtue, we eliminate its possibility. For by compelling everyone to bow to Mecca, we are preventing people from doing so out of freely adopted conviction. To be moral, an act must be free.

Frank Meyer put it eloquently in his *In Defense of Freedom*:

> ...freedom can exist at no lesser price than the danger of damnation; and if freedom is indeed the essence of man's being, that which distinguishes him from the beasts, he must be free to choose his worst as well as his best end. Unless he can choose his worst, he cannot *choose* his best.

And again:

> For moral and spiritual perfection can only be pursued by finite men through a series of choices, in which every moment is a new beginning; and freedom which makes those choices possible is itself a condition without which the moral and spiritual ends would be meaningless. If this were not so, if such ends could be achieved without the continuing exercise of freedom, then moral and spiritual perfection could be taught by rote and enforced by discipline—and every man of good will would be a saint. Freedom is therefore an integral aspect of the highest end.[1]

Freedom, in short, is a necessary but not sufficient condition for the achievement of virtue. With Lord Acton, we may say that freedom is the highest *political* end; in that subset of ethical principle that deals with the legitimacy of the use of violence between men, the libertarian—as well as the fusionist Meyer's—position holds that violence must be strictly limited to defending the freedom of individuals, their rights to person and property, against violent interference by others.

There is, then, nothing synthesizing about the "fusionist" position on this vital point; it is libertarian, period.

There is an odd aspect of the statist position on the enforcement of virtue that has gone unnoticed. It is bad enough, from the libertarian perspective, that the non-libertarian conservatives (along with all other breeds of statists) are eager to enforce compulsory virtue; but which group of men do they pick to do the enforcing? Which group in society are to be the guardians of virtue, the ones who define and enforce their vision of what virtue is supposed to be? None other, I would say, than the state apparatus, the social instrument of legalized violence. Now, even if we concede legitimate functions to the policeman, the soldier, the jailer, it is a peculiar vision that would entrust the guardianship of morality to a social group whose historical record for moral behavior is hardly encouraging.[2] Why should the sort of persons who are good at, and will therefore tend to exercise, the arts of shooting, gouging, and stomping, be the same persons we would want to select as our keepers of the moral flame? Hayek's brilliant chapter on "Why the Worst Get to the Top" applies not only to totalitarianism, but, in a lesser degree to be sure, to any attempts to enforce morality by means of the state:

> While we are likely to think that, since the desire for a collective system springs from high moral motives, such a system must be the breeding-ground for the

highest virtues, there is, in fact, no reason why any system should enhance those attitudes which serve the purpose for which it was designed. The ruling moral views will depend partly on qualities that will lead individuals to success in a collectivist or totalitarian system and partly on the requirements of the totalitarian machinery.[3]

It would seem far better, then, to entrust the guardianship of moral principles to organized bootblacks than to the professional wielders of violence who constitute the state apparatus.

If the state is to be the guardian and enforcer of morality, it follows that it should be the inculcator of moral principles as well. Among traditionalist conservatives, Walter Berns has been particularly dedicated to the idea of the nation-state as moulding and controlling the education of the youth, even going so far as to laud the work of Horace Mann. Meyer, on the other hand, was never more passionate in his libertarianism than when contemplating state education and the public school system—that mighty engine for the inculcation of "civic virtue." The responsibility for educating the young rests properly with the parent, the family, and not with the state.

If the fusionist position *is* simply the libertarian position on freedom-and-virtue, then what of the fusionist critique of libertarianism: that it ignores virtue altogether in the pursuit of freedom (or, at least, ignores virtue insofar as it goes beyond freedom itself)? Much of this critique rests on a fundamental misunderstanding of what libertarianism is all about. Thus, Professor John P. East spoke of the traditionalist concern about contemporary libertarianism (which he, as a fusionist, shared): "of taking a valid point, in this case the importance of the individual and his rights, and elevating it to the first principle of life with all other considerations excluded."(85) Even Frank Meyer, uncharacteristically and in the heat of the ideological fray, identified libertarianism as a "libertine impulse [which]...raises the freedom of the individual...to the status of an absolute end."[4] But this is an absurd straw-man. Only an imbecile could ever hold that freedom is the highest or indeed the only principle or end of life. Freedom is necessary to, and integral with, the achievement of any of man's ends. The libertarian agrees completely with Acton and with Meyer himself that freedom is the highest *political* end, not the highest end of man *per se*; indeed, it would be difficult to render such a position in any sense meaningful or coherent.

The confusion here, and the basic problem with conservatives' understanding of libertarianism, is that libertarianism *per se* does not offer a comprehensive way of life or system of ethics, as do, say, conservatism and Marxism. This does not mean in any sense that I am personally opposed to a comprehensive ethical system; quite the contrary. It simply means that libertarianism is strictly a *political* philosophy, confined to what the use of violence should be in social life. (As I have written above, libertarianism maintains that violence should be strictly limited to the defense of the rights of person and property against violent intervention.) Libertarianism does not talk about virtue in general (apart from the virtue of maintaining liberty), simply because it is not equipped to do so. As Professor Tibor Machan has pointed out, libertarianism is a "political doctrine...a claim as to what is permissible for human beings to do toward each other by means of the aid of force or its threat, nothing more."(105-106)

This does not mean that individual libertarians are unconcerned with moral principles or with broader philosophical issues. As a political theory, libertarianism is a coalition of adherents from all manner of philosophic (or non-philosophic) positions including emotivism, hedonism, Kantian *a priorism*, and many others. My own position grounds libertarianism on a natural rights theory embedded in a wider system of Aristotelian-Lockean natural law and a realist ontology and metaphysics.[5] But although those of us taking this position believe that it only provides a satisfactory groundwork and basis for individual liberty, this is an argument within the libertarian camp about the proper basis and grounding of libertarianism rather than about the doctrine itself.

More characteristic of Meyer was his identification of the libertarian pole of conservatism, not with liberty as the only goal for man, but with classical liberalism. Nineteenth-century liberalism rested its defense of liberty not on natural rights or moral principle, but on social utility and—in the case of the classical economists—economic efficiency. The classical liberal defense of liberty tended to be based not on the perception of freedom as essential to the true nature of man, but on universal ignorance of the truth. In some cases the approach is taken that knowledge of ethical truth would necessarily require coercion, so that freedom can only rest on the impossibility of knowing what virtuous action might be. In this way the classical liberal, or moral "libertine," agrees from the other side of the coin with the traditionalists: they acknowledge that if we only knew what the good might be we would have to enforce it upon everyone.[6]

Meyer's strictures against the utilitarian classical liberals were sound and well taken. As he put it, nineteenth-century liberalism "stood for individual freedom, but its utilitarian philosophical attitude denied the validity of moral ends firmly based on the constitution of being. Thereby, with this denial of an ultimate sanction for the inviolability of the person, liberalism destroyed the very foundations of its defense of the person as primary in political and social matters."[7] Meyer's mistake was in thinking that he was thereby indicting libertarianism *per se* when he was really attacking the classical liberal world-view underlying the underpinning for its own particular libertarian position. As Machan points out, "Classical liberalism may properly be regarded as far more than a political theory such as libertarianism, since it is philosophically broader, involving ideas about the nature of man, God, value, science, etc. Although libertarianism may indeed be defensible from a very specific philosophical perspective, it is not itself that perspective."(132)

Thus, Frank Meyer's strictures against libertarianism for neglecting virtue do not properly apply against libertarianism *per se*, since *qua* libertarianism it does not attempt to offer any theory except a political one; it is not competent to provide a general theory of ethics. His criticisms *do* properly apply to the broader ethical outlook of the utilitarian-emotivist-hedonic wing of libertarians, but not to the philosophy of the Aristotelian-Lockean natural rights wing. In other words, although he failed to realize it, Frank Meyer was writing, not as a fusionist attacking libertarianism, but as a natural law-natural rights libertarian attacking the philosophic perspective of the utilitarian-hedonic libertarians. In short, Meyer really wrote from within the libertarian perspective.

The utilitarian strain is particularly strong, in contemporary America, among the Chicago School wing of free-market economics: Milton Friedman, James Buchanan, Gordon Tullock, Ronald Coase, Harold Demsetz, et al. In recent decades, the assault of utilitarian "efficiency" upon ethics has reached almost grotesque proportions in the Chicago School economic theory of law advanced by Professor Richard Posner and his disciples. The Posnerites deny that law should have (or does have) anything to do with ethical principles; instead, the question of who should be considered a tortfeaser or liable for invading property rights should be decided purely on the basis of social "efficiency." Property rights themselves, according to the Chicagoites, should be allocated on the basis, not of justice, but of alleged efficiency considerations.[8] Indeed, some of the Chicagoite ventures, e.g., on economic analysis of sex and marriage, read like bizarre parodies of economics run riot, the sort of caricatures of economists in which Dickens was fond of indulging.[9]

For traditionalists the central object of concern and of imputed rights or obligations is the "community"; for libertarians it is the individual. For libertarians, communities are simply voluntary groupings of individuals, with no independent rights or powers of their own. The unit of analysis, the only entity that thinks, values, makes choices, is the individual. Again, there is no middle ground here; and, again, Frank Meyer's "fusionism" is squarely in the libertarian camp. Meyer began his *magnum opus* with methodological individualism; only individuals exist, and "society" is only an abstraction for a set of relations between them. A crucial error of twentieth-century thought, as Meyer pointed out, is that "the set of relationships between man itself constitutes a real entity—an organism, as it were—called 'society,' with a life and with moral duties and rights of its own. This hypostatization of the sum of relations between men, this calling into being of an organism as the value-center of political theory, is the essential note of the doctrines which underlie and inspire every powerful political movement of the 20th century...."[10]

So far, so good, and most conservatives as well as libertarians would agree. But then Meyer applied this analysis fully to the traditionalists' favored concept of "community":

> For "community" (except as it is freely created by free individual persons), community conceived as a principle of social order prior and superior to the individual person, can justify any oppression of individual persons so long as it is carried out in the name of "community" or society or of its agent, the state.

Meyer went on to warn that

> this is the principle of collectivism; and it remains the principle of collectivism even though the New Con-

servatives who speak of "community" would prefer a
congeries of communities...to the totalizing and
equalizing national or international community
which is the goal of the collectivists. This is to their
credit.... But what the New Conservatives will not see
is that there are no solid grounds on which the kind
of "community" they propose as the end towards
which social existence should be ordered can be defended against the kind of "community" the collectivists propose.... Caught within the pattern of concepts inherited from classical political theory, they
[the New Conservatives] cannot free themselves from
the doctrine that men find their true being only as
organic parts of a social entity, from which and in
terms of which their lives take value. Hence the New
Conservatives cannot effectively combat the essential political error of collectivist liberalism: its eleva-
tion of corporate society, and the state which stands
as the enforcing agency of corporate society, to the
level of final political ends.[11]

"Total state and 'plurality of communities,'" Meyer concluded, "do not constitute an antithesis; rather they are
variants...of the same denial of the primary value, on this
earth, of the individual person."[12]

The only genuine community among men, Meyer went
on to say, is the result of free and voluntary individual
interactions, not of the aridity and despotism of state-
imposed "community." The problems which traditionalists like Kirk and Nisbet ascribe to "loss of community,"
Meyer pointed out, really stem from "an excess of state-
enforced community."[13] In contrast, Meyer eloquently
held up associations of free persons:

To assert the freedom and independence of the individual person implies no denial of the value of mutuality, of association and common action between persons. It only denies the value of coerced association. When men are free, they will of course form among themselves a multitude of associations to fulfill common purposes when common purposes exist. The potential relationships between one man and other men are multifarious; but they are relationships between independent, conscious, self-acting beings. They are not the interactions of cells of a larger organism. When they are voluntary, freely chosen to fulfill the mutual needs of independent beings, they are fruitful and indeed essential. But...each man will find, as a free being, the relationships congenial to his specific needs.[14]

We conclude that, in this crucial area of political thought as well, Frank Meyer was not a "fusionist" but quite simply a trenchant individualist and libertarian. Always he championed the primacy of the individual, of his rights and liberty, as against all social institutions. Cooperation between men was fine, provided that it be free and voluntary; any coercion is a mockery of genuine community, and the state is particularly menacing whenever it goes beyond the use of force to guard individual rights against the coercion of others. This is no "third way," but simply libertarianism.

In choosing political or social positions, two alternatives have been offered: custom or tradition on the one hand, the use of reason to discern natural laws and rights on the other; in short, tradition, or the use of reason to discern abstract principles on which to stand one's ground outside the customs of time and place. Here, too, is a profound difference between traditionalist and libertarian. The traditionalist is at bottom an empiricist, distrusting rational abstraction and principle, and wrapping himself in the custom of his particular society. The libertarian, as Lord Acton stated, "wishes for what ought to be, irrespective of what is." Or, as Gertrude Himmelfarb has summed up Acton's viewpoint, "the past was allowed no authority except as it happened to conform to morality."[15]

Here again, Meyer came down basically on the libertarian side. Arguing against the traditionalists, he pointed out that there are many traditions; and how but by the use of reason can we decide between them? Time can hallow evil as well as good; it is no accident that the unreconstructed Stalinists in Russia were dubbed the "conservatives." Surely they were, in the traditionalist sense. But if we are stuck within tradition, whatever it may happen to be, how do we *know* whether it is good, indifferent, or evil? Only principle can judge, can decide between, traditions; and reason is our key to the discovery of principle. Meyer put it succinctly:

> Against both the prevailing mode of thought and the New Conservative criticism, which are, each in its own way, appeals to experience, I propose the claims of reason and the claims of the tradition of reason. I do not assume that reason is the sole possession of a single living generation, or of any man in any generation. I do assume that it is the active quality whereby men (starting with a due respect for the fundamental moral knowledge of ends and values incorporated in tradition) have the power to distinguish what ought to be from what is, the ideal from the dictates of

power. Upon these assumptions, I shall attempt to reestablish, in contemporary contexts, principles drawn from the nature of man....[16]

And again:

...there is a higher sanction than prescription and tradition; there are standards of truth and good by which men must make their ultimate judgment of ideas and institutions; in which case, reason, operating against the background of tradition, is the faculty upon which they must depend in making that judgment....To recognize that there is a need to distinguish between traditions, to choose between the good and the evil in tradition, requires recognition of the preeminent role (not, lest I be misunderstood, the sole role) of reason in distinguishing among the possibilities which have been open to men since the serpent tempted Eve.... But this is exactly what the New Conservatives refuse to recognize. The refusal to recognize the role of reason, the refusal to acknowledge that, in the immense flow of tradition, there are in fact diverse elements that must be distinguished on a principled basis...is a central attribute of New Conservative thought. It is this which separates the New Conservatism from the conservatism of principle....[17]

While I contend that Meyer's position is essentially libertarian, he evidently waffled in places in an uncharacteristically murky manner. If reason is needed to decide between traditions, to judge good and evil, in what sense does reason not have the "sole" role here? In other places, Meyer, with evident inconsistency, spoke of tradition as properly a "guide and governor of reason," or of reason operating "within tradition." Here, Meyer was trying desperately to establish a third, fusionist way between libertarianism and traditionalism, but at the price of inner contradiction and theoretical confusion. If reason is indispensable to judge good and evil and to decide between traditions, then obviously it cannot operate *within* tradition. For either reason is the ultimate arbiter, or tradition is; it is impossible to have it both ways. Fusionism has ineluctably run afoul of the law of the excluded middle (the product of reason, I might note).

Can we make any sense at all of Meyer's vague references to the proper role of tradition? Perhaps there is a clue in the clause, "starting with a due respect for the fundamental moral knowledge of ends and values incorporated in tradition." Perhaps this simply means that, if we wish to learn moral truth, we had better *begin* by finding out what the theorists of the present and past have had to say about it. This is not placing tradition above reason; it is simply employing common sense. If one wants to learn anything about the world, it saves time and energy, and adds a great number of insights, to say the least, to learn what has been written and thought on the subject, rather than each individual's attempting to spin out all knowledge from scratch. If Meyer or anyone else should think that the libertarian position is like Swift's spider, to spin everything out of one's head *a priori* without reference to thought of the past or present, then this would be only a bizarre caricature. Libertarians, one would hope, are intelligent human beings, and not solipsistic cretins.

Are there any other obeisances that libertarians may properly make to tradition? Simply to say that, in life, not *all* questions are matters of moral principle. There are numerous areas of life where people live by habit and custom, where the custom can neither be called moral or immoral, and where pursuit of custom eases the tensions of social life and makes for a more comfortable and harmonious society. It would be a false and perverted rationalism to say that any custom which cannot be proven on some other ground to be "rational" must go by the board. We can then conclude as follows: (a) that custom must be voluntarily upheld and not enforced by coercion; and (b) that people would be well advised (although not forced) to begin with a presumption in favor of custom, other things being equal. In a world, for example, where every man takes off his hat in the presence of ladies, an individual should be free not to do so, but at the risk of being generally judged a boor. If, on the other hand, this person's constitution is such that he would be likely to suffer a bad cold by exposing his pate, then we have here a higher moral consideration overriding the social harmonies of custom.

Returning to Frank Meyer, I still believe that the basic thrust of his fusionism in this dispute, as incoherent as it ultimately may be, is libertarian. Reason turns out to be decisive, and it seems to me that the bows to tradition are more ceremonial than substantive. I suspect, without being able to prove it, that Meyer was bowing here to what he deeply felt to be the exigencies of organizing a conservative movement which would include traditionalists, libertarians, fusionists. In short, that in this as in some other instances, Meyer was writing with a movement, rather than strictly intellectual exigencies, in mind.

Meyer has a sensitive discussion of Burke which I think

is relevant here. In discussing the ambiguities in Burke's thought between principle and prescription—the very problem here under discussion—he at one point explains the prescriptive side as emanating from Burke the statesman. The New Conservative disciples of Burke, Meyer points out, "are not statesmen like Burke; the prudential choice between immediate practical alternatives, which is the proper task of the statesman, leads in the scholar, the political theorist, to a theoretical impasse."[18]

I submit that, on this particular issue, Meyer was writing as a statesman instead of a political theorist.[19]

Another reason that I believe Meyer to be at heart a libertarian on this issue of principle vs. tradition is the stance he took on the related question of radical change vs. maintenance of the status quo. For as the post-New Deal system becomes ensconced in American life, many conservatives have increasingly become content to retain that system and simply to tinker with marginal reform. In a sense as good traditionalists, they aspire only to preserve the essential status quo and to keep the society from becoming *more* collectivist and more egalitarian than it already is. But Frank Meyer would have none of this. Until the end of his life he insisted on pursuing the unswerving goal of repealing the New Deal system root and branch, in fact, of repealing most of the accretions of statism in American life since the Civil War. Meyer's famous bitter critiques of Abraham Lincoln were not simply exercises in antiquarian disputation, nor of course were they defenses of racism and slavery.[20] Meyer saw clearly that the changes Lincoln wrought in American society were the decisive shift toward the centralizing and despotic nation-state, changes that were built upon by the Progressive era, by Woodrow Wilson, and finally by the New Deal. To Meyer, the goal of a truly principled conservative movement was to repeal all that, and to establish a just polity.

But this means that Meyer was truly a radical conservative, that is, someone who desired root and systematic change; he was in radical opposition to the statist status quo. Hence he took his stand, once again, with the libertarians, who are also principled radicals, and with much the same principles.

Another critical dispute between traditionalists and libertarians is over the role and the nature of order. To the traditionalist, order is the overriding consideration, and order can only be achieved by a massive imposition of state coercion. To the traditionalist, liberty is arrant chaos and disorder, and the libertarian is someone who wishes to sacrifice order on the altar of liberty. The libertarian, on the contrary, has a diametrically opposed view. To him, the only genuine order among men proceeds out of free and voluntary interaction: a lasting order that emerges out of liberty rather than by suppressing it. With Proudhon, the libertarian hails Liberty as the "Mother, not the Daughter of Order." In this way, the libertarian sees the harmonious interaction of free people as akin to the harmonious interaction of natural entities that is summed up as "natural law."

State coercion, on the other hand, is viewed by the libertarian as a pseudo-order which actually results in disorder and chaos. State-imposed order is "artificial" and destructive of the harmony provided by following the natural order. Economic science has long shown that individuals, pursuing their own interests in the marketplace, will benefit everyone. The free market has been shown to be the only genuine economic order, while state coercion hampering that market only subverts genuine order and causes dislocation, general impoverishment and, eventually, economic chaos. Moreover, one of our most distinguished free-market economists, F. A. Hayek, has extended the concept of what he has trenchantly termed "spontaneous order" to include many other activities than the economic sphere.[21] Hayek has pointed out that the evolution of human language itself was not imposed by coercion from above but emerged from the free and voluntary interaction of individual persons. To use a noted phrase of Hayek's, language, the origin of money, and the market itself were products or byproducts of human action, but not of human design.

An eloquent statement of the libertarian view of order was given us by Paine:

> A great part of that order which reigns among mankind is not the effect of government. It had its origin in the principles of society and the natural constitution of man. It existed prior to government, and would exist if the formality of government was abolished. The mutual dependence and reciprocal interest which man has upon man, and all parts of a civilized community upon each other, create that great chain of connection which holds it together. The landholder, the farmer, the manufacturer, the merchant, the tradesman, and every occupation, prospers by the aid which each receives from the other, and from the whole. Common interest regu-

lates their concerns, and forms their laws; and the laws which common usage ordains, have a greater influence than the laws of government. In fine, society performs for itself almost every thing which is ascribed to government.[22]

As to Frank Meyer, it is clear throughout his work that he believes in the order of liberty rather than in state coercion. In reply to the traditionalists, he points out that *all* social systems have *some sort* of order, and that the relevant question, then, is not: order or no order? but *what kind* of order?[23] The order he evidently believes in is one of freedom: of the protection of the rights of person and property, and of a free market economy—in short, the order of libertarianism. Once again, "fusionism" turns out to be libertarianism in another guise.

Finally, a fascinating problem within conservatism transcends the traditionalist-fusionist-libertarian triad altogether, and furnishes an example of the triad's insufficiency in encompassing problems within conservative thought. Broadly, this is the question of "populism" vs. "elitism," that is, does one pin one's hopes for proper social change and a just society on the mass of the public or on an elite minority? Or, to put it another way, who is The Enemy? Which social groups or institutions constitute the permanent menace and enemy to be combatted and guarded against?

Originally, the traditionalists (Kirk, Viereck, Wilhelmsen, et al.) could be placed squarely in the elitist camp. The masses were The Enemy, as I see their views, and a strong state and repressive institutions headed by the state were needed to keep the masses in check. The result was an inherent pessimism about the future. For, since the late nineteenth century, the masses have voted, and therefore the conservative cause has seemed ineluctably doomed.[24]

Libertarians, on the other hand, tended to be far more populist. To libertarians, the masses are not The Enemy. The Enemy, in the dramatic terms of Spencer and Nock, is the state. This does not mean that libertarians naively believe that the masses are necessarily wise or good. It is simply that the mass of the public spends most of its time on the business of making a living; their political interests are fitful and evanescent. At their worst, the masses may conduct a lynching or two, but then they are back to their daily affairs. But the state consists of full-time professionals in coercion. It is the business of the state apparatus never to rest. So the state, rather than the masses, is the permanent Enemy. This has meant, in the libertarian tradition, that either the state is to be abolished, or, if retained, that it be kept small and weighed down with fierce restrictions and greeted by permanent social hostility. Jefferson's "eternal vigilance [as] the price of liberty" was directed against the state.[25]

But it is not just that libertarians direct their fire against the state. They also perceive that the masses, as well as numerous individuals, are oppressed by the state, that the state benefits a minority power elite at the expense of most of those it purports to help. In the late 70s and 80s, as part of this analysis, economists began documenting how the poor are injured rather than helped by the welfare state. But further, statism deeply violates the basic laws of man's nature. For, if the state's interest really clashes with the majority of the people, with their freedom, happiness and prosperity, then education of the masses in this truth will be likely to result eventually in libertarian victory, a victory which would replicate and extend the partial victories of their classical liberal forebears in the eighteenth and nineteenth centuries.

The original correlation of traditionalist with the elite and libertarian with populism, however, has long been swept away. Since the 1960s, traditionalist conservatives have become increasingly pro-populist, culminating in the New Right. Partly, as George Nash indicates in his history of the modern conservative movement, the shift in attitude toward the masses reflected a change in historical context. In the 1940s and 1950s conservatives were an embattled minority, and so saw themselves as an eternally beleaguered group fending off both state and mass. But as conservatives began to grow and achieve political victories in the 1960s and 1970s, their attitude toward the masses swung one hundred eighty degrees, and we began to hear of a "silent majority" who knew in their hearts that conservatism was right.[26] In addition, such new traditionalists as the late Willmoore Kendall stressed the virtually absolute "rights" of the putative majority of the public.

Late in the 1970s, New Right publicist Jude Wanniski attained the apotheosis of populism. As with Kendall, Wanniski and New Right populism far exceeded the libertarian bent, which is only a long-run tendency, and which denies the majority any power to interfere with the rights of the individual. Wanniski went to the extent of declaring, in some sort of Hegelian fashion, that history consists of the masses fulfilling their will. In striking contrast to the original traditionalists as well as to libertarians, Wanniski proclaimed that the masses never need to be educated; on the contrary, they are all-wise. The masses, at any time in history, know all. The task of political leadership is to articulate the wisdom of the masses and to bring them what they want, since what they want is always wise and right. Specifically, Wanniski saw the cunning of history as marching inevitably toward (a) a world state, and (b) greater and greater democracy. Democracy becomes a positive and overriding good, in this view, because it more easily fulfills the inevitably wise and good desires of the masses.[27]

In the face of this ultra-populism, the libertarian position is quite modest and commonsensical. It holds that the long-run interest of the masses and their basic human nature, is, in reality, opposed to statism, but this hardly guarantees instantaneous or even eventual success. It certainly doesn't imply the eternal wisdom of the general public.

As far as I know, Frank Meyer never addressed himself specifically to this question, but I think that his basic position was close to the libertarian one. Democracy was cogently criticized, and warned against as a menace to liberty, but so too was the State as well as more particular "communities." Probably Meyer, along with most other conservatives, grew more optimistic about the masses as conservatism gained political strength, but so far as that goes this is both an understandable and proper response to changing political realities. The point is that, holding the liberty and the rights of the individual as paramount, Meyer would never have succumbed to the adoration of the

masses recently so prevalent in the conservative movement. Once again, even though the familiar triad is not very
helpful here, Meyer's "fusionist" position is basically libertarian.

I conclude from a study of its founder and leading exponent that "fusionism" does not really exist. In all the crucial
aspects of political philosophy, Frank Meyer was a libertarian. There is no triad, but only two very different and largely
antagonistic poles. In the one area where Meyer differed
substantively from the libertarian position, reason as being
"within tradition," I submit that the attempt was so baldly
fallacious that it can only be explained as a heroic or
desperate (depending on one's point of view) attempt to
find a face-saving formula to hold both very different parts
of the conservative movement together in a unified ideological and political movement. To use Marxian jargon,
fusionism often seems like an attempt to paper over the
contradictions within conservatism. I venture to assert
that, if we were living in a very different kind of society
where there was no political strife or movements, and
political disputes were strictly confined to political theory
in the cloistered groves of academe, there would have been
no fusionism and Meyer would have acknowledged himself
as a libertarian, of the natural rights variety. In short, I
believe that fusionism is a "myth" in the Sorelian sense, an
organizing principle to hold two very disparate wings of a
political movement together and to get them to act in a
unified way. Intellectually, the concept must be judged a
failure.

Notes

1. Frank S. Meyer, *In Defense of Freedom* (Chicago: Henry Regnery, 1962), 50, 55.
2. For the historical record of the criminality of rulers of state, see Pitirim A. Sorokin and Walter A. Lunden, *Power and Morality: Who Shall Guard the Guardians?* (Boston: Porter Sargent, 1959).
3. Friedrich A. Hayek, *The Road to Serfdom* (Chicago: University of Chicago Press, 1944), 136.
4. Frank S. Meyer, "Libertarianism or Libertinism?," *National Review* 21 (Sept. 9, 1969): 910.
5. This is essentially the position of Tibor Machan, Eric Mack, Douglas Rasmussen, Douglas den Uyl, Williamson Evers, Randy E. Barnett, Anthony Fressola, George H. Smith, and a host of other libertarian political philosophers.
6. The free market economist Milton Friedman, from the classical liberal perspective, has explicitly taken that very position. See Machan's essay in this volume, "Libertarianism"(110).
7. Meyer, *Defense*, 1-2.
8. Thus see Richard A. Posner, *Economic Analysis of Law*, 2nd ed. (Boston: Little Brown, 1977); Posner, "Utilitarianism, Economics, and Legal Theory," *Journal of Legal Studies* 8 (January 1979): 103-40; Harold B. Demsetz, "Ethics and Efficiency in Property Rights Systems," in Mario J. Rizzo, ed., *Time, Uncertainty, and Disequilibrium* (Lexington, Mass: Lexington Books, 1979), 97-116. For critiques of Chicagoite Posnerism from a rights-perspective, see Ronald M. Dworkin, "Is Wealth a Value?," *Journal of Legal Studies* (March 1980): 191-226; Richard A. Epstein, "The Static Conception of the Common Law," *ibid.*, 253-76; Rizzo, "Law Amid Flux: The Economics of Negligence and Strict Liability in Tort," *ibid.*, 291-318; Charles Fried, "The Laws of Change: The Cunning of Reason in Moral and Legal History," *ibid.*, 335-53; Gerald P. O'Driscoll, Jr., "Justice, Efficiency, and the Economic Analysis of Law: A Comment on Fried," *ibid.*, 355-56; John B. Egger, "Comment: Efficiency is Not a Substitute for Ethics," in Rizzo, ed., *op. cit.*, 117-26; Rizzo, "Uncertainty, Subjectivity, and the Economic Analysis of Law," *ibid.*, 71-90; Murray N. Rothbard, "The Myth of Efficiency," *ibid.*, 91-96.
9. For an example, see Richard B. McKenzie and Gordon Tullock, *The New World of Economics: Explorations into the Human Experience* (Homewood,

Ill.: Richard D. Irwin, 1975). Actually, Wilde's quip about the cynic applies equally well to these Chicagoite economists: they "who know the price of everything, and the value of nothing."

10. Meyer, *Defense*, 28.

11. *Ibid.*, 130-32.

12. *Ibid.*, 144.

13. *Ibid.*, 130.

14. *Ibid.*, 146-47. For a penetrating critique of the worship of the *polis* as against individual persons in classical political theory, see *ibid.*, 82-87, 136.

15. Gertrude Himmelfarb, *Lord Acton: A Study in Conscience and Politics* (Chicago: University of Chicago Press, 1962), 204-05. Or, as one philosopher has defined natural law: it "defends the rational dignity of the human individual and his right and duty to criticize by word and deed any existent institution of social structure in terms of those universal moral principles which can be apprehended by the individual intellect alone." John Wild, *Plato's Modern Enemies and the Theory of Natural Law* (Chicago: University of Chicago Press, 1953), 176.

16. Meyer, *Defense*, 11.

17. *Ibid.*, 41, 44-45.

18. *Ibid.*, 40.

19. I do not write this to denigrate Frank Meyer the man. It is certainly arguable that organizing and leading an ideological movement may be just as admirable as constructing an edifice of political theory. Meyer was a committed man, as well as a theorist and scholar; he was not content only to discover good and evil. Believing that twentieth-century man had taken a tragically wrong road, he believed it his duty to organize to change that road. He believed it incumbent upon him to act on his theoretical insights.

20. Frank S. Meyer, "Lincoln Without Rhetoric," *National Review* 17 (Aug. 24, 1965): 725; idem., "Again on Lincoln," *National Review* 18 (Jan. 25, 1966): 71, 85.

21. See in particular F. A. Hayek, *Law, Legislation, and Liberty*, Vol. 1: *Rules and Order* (Chicago: University of Chicago Press, 1973). Perhaps the earliest use of the phrase "spontaneous order," where the concept is developed much as Hayek would do later, and applied to the diffusion of scientific knowledge, is in Michael Polanyi, *The Logic of Liberty* (Chicago: University of Chicago Press, 1951).

22. Thomas Paine, "Rights of Man, Part Second," in P. Foner, ed., *The Complete Writings of Thomas Paine* (New York: Citadel Press, 1945), 1: 357.

23. Thus, see Meyer, *Defense*, 64-65.

24. Among Chicago free-market economists, George Stigler has come to the position that liberty is irretrievably doomed so long as universal suffrage exists. Since the prospects for repealing universal suffrage seem about as favorable as for the restoration of the Stuarts, pessimism becomes inevitable.

25. For the influence of *Cato's Letters* and other radical English libertarians of this stripe on the American revolutionaries, see Bernard Bailyn, *The Ideological Origins of the American Revolution* (Cambridge, Mass.: Belknap Press of Harvard University Press, 1967).

26. George H. Nash, *The Conservative Intellectual Movement in America Since 1945* (Wilmington, Dela.: Intercollegiate Studies Institute, 1996).

27. Jude Wanniski, *The Way the World Works* (New York: Simon and Schuster, 1978). On the evidence of the book, the point of all this seems to be specifically political: that is, to argue why a Republican Presidential candidate who calls for tax reduction, maintenance of government spending at the current level, *and* a balanced budget is not being an irresponsible demagogue. He is not because the masses, on the evidence of Gallup polls, etc., want all three, and therefore they must be right. It is the task of conservative intellectuals to find out why they are right, and it is at this point that Wanniski brings in the *deus ex machina* of the "Laffer curve," which purports to resolve these contradictions. But in this paper we are concerned only with the historical-theoretical underpinnings for this political gimcrackery.

Differences of Theory and Strategy

JOHN HOSPERS

The popular mythology has it that libertarians agree with conservatives on economic matters but differ from them on personal liberties. Although there is some truth in this formulation, it is an oversimplification; it conceals the many nuances of likeness and difference that exist.

Libertarians have many diverse moral and religious views, but as far as their political philosophy is concerned they are united in a tolerance for different moralities and different life-styles as long as these are practiced non-coercively. The watchword of libertarian thought on this matter was uttered by Herbert Spencer in 1848 when he set forth what he called "the law of equal freedom": "Each man should be free to act as he chooses, provided he trenches not on the equal freedom of each other man to act as he chooses." Many libertarians believe that, since government is by nature coercive, all governments violate these freedoms, and as a result they are anarchists; other libertarians believe that a properly limited government (one limited to the retaliatory use of force) would not do so, and that even if it does to some extent the reign of law is worth the small price in liberty; consequently, they are advocates of limited government, the "night watchman" view of government which limits its function to protection and defense. This issue divides libertarians, and I shall not go into it here. In any case, libertarians are dedicated to freedom of choice except the choice to coerce: they agree that adults have a right to engage in whatever non-coercive activities they wish, such as sexual activity of whatever kind between consenting parties and the ingestion of drugs, even dangerous drugs.

There are, however, numerous gray areas in the application of this rule which have not to my mind been adequately worked out by libertarians. Becoming intoxicated at home is all right, driving while intoxicated is not because of the danger to everyone on the highway (I know of only a few libertarians who would not wish a drunk driver to be arrested until after the accident has occurred). Raising poisonous snakes on your private island is all right, raising them in your backyard in the city is not, because of the danger it presents to others. I should think that in all consistency libertarians would also distinguish among drugs in the same way: the use of heroin makes one passive and not a danger to anyone else (the danger to others results from the illegality of the product, causing its price to skyrocket, and leading people to burglarize apartments to raise money for the fix), but the use of PCP can turn one into a madman, a danger to everyone in the vicinity. But I have not heard libertarians make a case against the use of the latter drug.

Libertarians do agree that if there is to be a legal crime there must be a victim, and insist that sex laws and drug laws make victimless crimes—but it would seem to me that the use of some drugs makes many people potential victims in exactly the same way as drunken driving does (not to mention the families of addicts, who are victims also). (But of course, in exactly the same way, the families of felons are victims, and may suffer more from the husband's incarceration than he does; yet we do not on that account refrain from imprisoning felons.) Libertarians will agree, in any case, that the law is not there to protect people from themselves, but only from other people—and that no matter how harmful the drug or the drink is to the person, he is entitled to use it as long as he does not endanger others. The question to be asked, then, is to what degree must he endanger others before his activity should be prohibited? The question is a general one, with thousands of applications. Is having a pond in one's backyard, unfenced, a danger because trespassers might swim and drown in it? Is having a fence around one's property with a slight bit of electricity coursing through it to deter trespassers also to be considered a danger to others?

The libertarian answers to such questions are far from clear. But even less clear is what libertarians would say when there is not actual danger of *harm*, but simply of *offense*. Would all libertarians favor X-rated movies? Would they favor allowing under age persons to see them? Would they favor obscene photos displayed on billboards so that they can escape no one's view? Would they favor the legalization of nudity in parks and beaches, not to mention one's own yard? Many of these things can not very plausibly be said to *harm* others, but simply to *offend* and embarrass others. Now if libertarians believe that everything should be permitted except what harms others, where do these things fall? I have heard of a right not to be killed or tortured, a right not to be harmed; is there also a right not to be offended? I think that some room must be made for restrictions on the public display of what (at least) the vast majority of people find offensive, but I cannot find any justification in the corpus of libertarian theory for this.

Another gray area is the problem of mental incompetents. Libertarians are vigorously anti-paternalistic: paternalism is doing something for another person's benefit but against that person's will. Many libertarians oppose the rule that a policeman must attempt to rescue someone who tries to drown himself in the river. They would say that if a person wants to kill himself he should be permitted to do so. If a hospital patient refuses to eat, don't make him eat, let him die if that's what he wants. The problem with this is that by acceding to the patient's wishes at time t-1 he may be going against them at time t-2, t-3, etc. The attendant may force-feed the patient, and the patient may later thank him for saving his life. Should one accede to that person's wishes at one time, whatever they are, if by doing so he frustrates them at another? If the 90-year-old-couple, now somewhat lapsed into senility, refuse to pay the utility bills, would the libertarian say, "If they want to be in the cold and the dark, let them," or would he do what most children of such elderly people do, get a power of attorney to sign their checks and keep them warm? There are countless possible cases for legal paternalism in this area, each with its own individual variations.

The problem of the rights of children has long been a thorny issue. Libertarians are all for children's rights, for their right to leave home before 18, to take responsibility for their own actions, to sign contracts and go to bars. But to give children these same rights at 8 instead of 18 would be quite absurd—and the same question arises for libertarians as for those who are more comfortable with legal paternalism, as to where to draw the line with all this. Some children are more mature at 14 than others are at 18, and the same child may have a mature judgment in one respect and not in another. In this area the libertarian might place the age of consent a little earlier than others would, but even so he would confront the same problems as have vexed legislators on the issue from time immemorial.

Again, libertarians vociferously oppose the non-voluntary commitment of anyone to mental institutions; if he is accused of a crime let him stand trial, and if he is not, let him go no matter how kooky he seems to others. The mere fact that one is judged idiosyncratic or a bit loony by others is no reason for commitment, that is, for depriving someone of his rights and keeping him imprisoned in an institution, possibly for years. But there is another consideration that cuts across this one, to which libertarians have not sufficiently addressed themselves: what if the person is *dangerous* to others? Whatever makes a person "mentally incompetent" (and there is no uniform opinion on this) should not be reason for his incarceration; but whatever makes him dangerous is, whether he be found insane or not. Danger to others is difficult to judge, yet it is of the utmost importance, for the same reason that drunk driving statutes are: if you don't have them there are going to be lots of victims.

To the conservative, I suspect, all this is too permissive. Some conservatives, but not all, would pass laws prohibiting sexual relations outside of marriage even by consenting adults; almost all conservatives would ban hard drugs entirely, and some soft ones as well. Many conservatives, though not all, would use the authority of the state to steer the nation in a pro-Christian mold, or at least pro-Judeo-Christian, such as by prayer in schools, the encouragement of certain teachings, and sometimes the banning of others. They would do this paternalistically, so that the level of public morality would be higher, and so that the work ethic and the religious traditions of the founding fathers might be better preserved in our time, as well as to preserve a high level of public religious morality in our culture. Many libertarians would applaud some or all of these goals, but they would not approve the means suggested for doing it: they would say that all such goals should be worked for and achieved through cooperative *voluntary* institutions such as schools and churches and that this essential voluntariness precludes any interference by the state.

The lines between the libertarian and conservative positions were already drawn on this issue a century ago. John Stuart Mill wrote, in *On Liberty*, "Neither one person, nor any number of persons, is warranted in saying to another human being of ripe years, that he shall not do with his life for his own benefit what he chooses to do with it...the only purpose for which power can be rightfully exercised over any member of a civilized community, against his will, is to prevent harm to others. He cannot rightfully be compelled to do or forbear because it will be better for him to do so, because it will make him happier, because in the opinion of others, to do so would be wise, or even right." And Mill added: "A man's mode of laying out his existence is the best, not because it is best in itself, but because it is his own mode.... It is the privilege and proper condition of a human being, arrived at the maturity of his faculties, to use and interpret experience in his own way."

But Mill's nearly total attack on coercion was opposed by his contemporary Fitzjames Stephen, in his book *Liberty, Equality, Fraternity* (1892), who thought that the use of coercion was often important for achieving social ends:

> The question whether liberty is a good or a bad thing appears as irrational as the question whether fire is a good or a bad thing. It is both good and bad according to time, place, and circumstances....
> Compulsion is bad—
> (1) when the object aimed at is bad.
> (2) when the object aimed at is good, but the compulsion employed is not calculated to obtain it;
> (3) when the object aimed at is good, and the compulsion employed is calculated to obtain it, but at too great an expense.
> Thus, to compel a man to commit murder is bad, because the object is bad.
> To inflict a punishment sufficient to irritate but not sufficient to deter or to destroy for holding particular religious opinions is bad, because such compulsion is not calculated to effect its purpose, assuming it to be good.
> To compel people not to trespass by shooting them with spring-guns is bad, because the harm done is out of all proportion to the harm avoided.

> If, however, the object aimed at is good, if the compulsion employed such as to attain it, and if the good obtained overbalances the inconvenience of the compulsion itself, I do not understand how...the compulsion can be bad.

Even a libertarian, I think, believing though he does in freedom of contract, would balk at admitting the validity of a contract in which a person consented to be someone else's slave for life. It would be an exercise of his freedom of such a kind as to ensure that he had no more freedom from that point on. I hope he would also balk at the example of a motorist who inquires of another how to get across a certain bridge, and the other person, knowing that the other end of the bridge has been washed away in a flood, purposely refrains from giving the inquirer this information. I hope also that he would not honor the contract of a patient in a hospital to engage in some new medical experiment without being told the possible dangerous side-effects of the new drug; surely he would have to implement his stock phrase "by mutual voluntary consent" to read "by mutual voluntary and *informed* consent." Perhaps, though this is pressing one's luck, he could also be talked into approving an enforced waiting period for teenage marriages.

Though I am inclined to agree with the general libertarian approach, I would take a rather conservative view in the gray areas. Children cannot be cut loose too soon without great harm to themselves; a 23-year-old should be free to accept or reject a sexual offer, but not a 13-year-old. An adult may try a drug if doing so is no danger to others, but a child, unaware of the full possible consequences of his action, may not. And self-destructive contracts should not be honored. Freedom is a great thing, but one should not run the danger of destroying oneself in the pursuit of it.

A Dispassionate Assessment
of Libertarians

RUSSELL KIRK

The term *libertarianism* is distasteful to people who think
seriously about politics. Both Dr. F. A. Hayek and your
servant have gone out of their way, from time to time, to
declare that they refuse to be tagged with this label. Anyone
much influenced by the thought of Edmund Burke and of
Alexis de Tocqueville—as were both Professor Hayek and
this commentator—sets his face against ideology; and
libertarianism is a simplistic ideology, relished by one
variety of the folk whom Burckhardt called "the terrible
simplifiers."

Nevertheless, I have something to say, just now, favorable to today's libertarians in the United States; later I shall
dwell upon their vices. With your indulgence, I will make
three points about persons calling themselves libertarians
that may warm the cockles of their rebellious hearts.

First, a number of the men and women who accept the
label "libertarian" are not actually ideological libertarians
at all, but simply conservatives under another name. These

are people who perceive in the growth of the monolithic state, especially during the past half-century, a grim menace to ordered liberty; and of course they are quite right. They wish to emphasize their attachment to personal and civic freedom by employing this twentieth-century word derived from *liberty*. With them I have little quarrel—except that by so denominating themselves, they seem to countenance a crowd of political fantastics who "license they mean when they cry liberty."

For if a man believes in an enduring moral order, the Constitution of the United States, established American ways of life, and a free economy—why, actually he is a conservative, even if he labors under an imperfect understanding of the general terms of politics. Such Americans are to the conservative movement in the United States much as the Liberal Unionists have been to the Conservative Party in Britain—that is, close practical allies, almost indistinguishable nowadays. Libertarians of this description usually are intellectual descendants of the old "classical liberals"; they make common cause with regular conservatives against the menace of democratic despotism and economic collectivism.

Second, the libertarians generally—both the folk of whom I have just approved, and also the ideological libertarians—try to exert some check upon vainglorious foreign policy. They do not believe that the United States should station garrisons throughout the world; no more do I; in some respects, the more moderate among them have the understanding of foreign policy that the elder Robert Taft represented. Others among them, however, seem to labor under the illusion that communist ideology can be dissipated by trade agreements—a notion really fatuous. I lack time to labor this point here; I shall take it up again elsewhere when I discuss the Neo-Conservatives, who in foreign policy tend toward an opposite extreme. Let it suffice for the present for me to declare that so far as the libertarians set their faces against a policy of American domination worldwide—why, I am with them. I part with them when they forget that the American government nowadays, in Burke's phrase of two centuries ago, is "combating an armed doctrine," not merely a national adversary.

Third, most of the libertarians believe in the humane scale; they vehemently oppose what Wilhelm Roepke called "the cult of the colossal." They take up the cause of the self-reliant individual, the voluntary association, the just rewards of personal achievement. They know the perils of political centralization. In an age when many folk are ready—nay, eager—to exchange their independence for "entitlements," the libertarians exhort us to stand manfully on our own feet.

In short, the libertarians' propaganda, which abounds, does touch upon real social afflictions of our time, particularly upon repression of vigorous and aspiring natures by centralized political structures and by the enforcement of egalitarian doctrines. With reason, many people in many lands, near the end of the twentieth century, are discontented with the human condition; the more able among the discontented look about for some seemingly logical alternative to present dominations and powers; and some of those discontented—the sort of people who went out to David in the Cave of Adullam—discover libertarian dogmata and become enthusiasts, at least temporarily, for the ideology called libertarianism.

I say *temporarily*: for an initial fondness for libertarian slogans frequently has led young men and women to the conservative camp. Not a few of the people who have studied closely with me or who have become my assistants had been attracted, a few years earlier, to the arguments of Ayn Rand or of Murray Rothbard. But as they read more widely, they had become conscious of the inadequacies and extravagances of the various libertarian factions; as they had begun to pay serious attention to our present political difficulties, they had seen how impractical are the libertarian proposals. Thus they had found their way to conservative realism, which proclaims that politics is the art of the possible. Therefore it may be said of libertarianism, in friendly fashion, that often it has been a recruiting-office for young conservatives, even though the libertarians have had not the least intention of shoring up belief in custom, convention, and the politics of prescription.

There! I have endeavored to give the libertarians their due. Now let me turn to their failings, which are many and grave.

For the ideological libertarians are not conservatives in any true meaning of that term of politics; nor do the more candid libertarians desire to be called conservatives. On the contrary, they are radical doctrinaires, contemptuous of our inheritance from our ancestors. They rejoice in the radicalism of Tom Paine; they even applaud those seventeenth-century radicals the Levellers and the Diggers, who would have pulled down all land-boundaries, and have pulled down, too, the whole framework of church and state. The libertarian groups differ on some points among themselves, and exhibit varying degrees of fervor. But one may say of them in general that they are "philosophical" anarchists in bourgeois dress. Of society's old institutions, they would retain only private property. They seek an abstract Liberty that never has existed in any civilization— nor, for that matter, among any barbarous people, nor any savage. They would sweep away political government; in this, they subscribe to Marx's notion of the withering away of the state.

One trouble with this primitive understanding of freedom is that it could not possibly work in twentieth-century America. The American Republic, and the American industrial and commercial system, require the highest degree of cooperation that any civilization ever has known. We prosper because most of the time we work together—and are restrained from our appetites and passions, to some extent, by laws enforced by the state. We need to limit the state's powers, of course, and our national Constitution does that—if not perfectly, at least more effectively than does any other national constitution.

The Constitution of the United States distinctly is not an exercise in libertarianism. It was drawn up by an aristocratic body of men who sought "a more perfect union." The delegates to the Constitutional Convention had a wholesome dread of the libertarians of 1786-87, as represented by the rebels who followed Daniel Shays in Massachusetts. What the Constitution established was a higher degree of order and prosperity, not an anarchists' paradise. So it is somewhat amusing to find some old gentlemen and old ladies who contribute heavily to the funds of the libertarian organizations in the mistaken belief that thus they are helping to restore the virtuous freedom of the early Republic. American industry and commerce on a large scale could not survive for a single year, without the protections extended by government at its several levels.

"To begin with unlimited freedom," Dostoevsky wrote, "is to end with unlimited despotism." The worst enemies of enduring freedom for all may be certain folk who demand incessantly more liberty for themselves. This is true of a country's economy, as of other matters. America's economic success is based upon an old foundation of moral habits, social customs and convictions, much historical experience, and commonsensical political understanding. Our structure of free enterprise owes much to the conservative understanding of property and production expounded by Alexander Hamilton—the adversary of the libertarians of his day. But our structure of free enterprise owes nothing at all to the destructive concept of liberty that devastated Europe during the era of the French Revolution—that is, to the ruinous impossible freedom preached by Jean Jacques Rousseau. Our twentieth-century libertarians are disciples of Rousseau's notion of human nature and Rousseau's political doctrines.

Have I sufficiently distinguished between libertarians and conservatives? Here I have been trying to draw a line of demarcation, not to refute libertarian arguments; I shall turn to the latter task very soon.

Before I essay that task, however, let me illustrate my discourse by a parable.

The typical libertine of 1998 delights in eccentricity—in private life as in politics. His is the sort of freedom, or license, that brings on social collapse. Libertarianism and libertinism are near allied. As that staunch Victorian conservative James Fitzjames Stephen instructs us, "Eccentricity is far more often a mark of weakness than a mark of strength." G. K. Chesterton remarks that true genius is not eccentric, but centric.

With respect to libertarian eccentricity, their dream of an absolute private freedom is one of those visions which issue from between the gates of ivory; and the disorder that they would thrust upon society already is displayed in the moral disorder of their private affairs. Some keen readers will recall the article on libertarianism in *National Review*, a few years ago, by that mordant psychologist and sociologist Dr. Ernest van den Haag, who remarked that an unusually high proportion of professed libertarians are homosexuals. In politics as in private life, they demand what nature cannot afford.

The enemy to all custom and convention ends in the outer darkness, where there is wailing and gnashing of teeth. The final emancipation from religion, the state, moral and positive law, and social responsibilities is total annihilation: the freedom of deadly destruction. When obsession with an abstract Liberty has overcome personal and public order—why, then, in Eliot's lines, we are

> ...*whirled*
> *Beyond the circuit of the shuddering Bear*
> *In fractured atoms.*

Just that is the theme of my parable—or rather, of

Chesterton's parable, for I offer you now a hasty synopsis of G. K. Chesterton's story "The Yellow Bird"—which too few people have read, though it was published in 1929. Chesterton knew that we must accept the universe that was created for us.

In Chesterton's tale, there comes to a venerable English country house a guest, Professor Ivanhov, a Russian scholar who has published a much-praised book, *The Psychology of Liberty*. He is a zealot for emancipating, expanding, the elimination of all limits—in short, a thoroughgoing libertarian.

Ivanhov, under the shelter of an old English roof and enjoying not merely all English liberties but also the privileges of a guest, proceeds to put into practice his libertarian doctrines. He commences his operations by liberating the yellow bird, a canary, from its cage; once out the window, the canary is harassed by the wild birds of the woods. The next day Ivanhov proceeds to liberate his host's goldfish by smashing their bowl. On the third day, resolved not to endure imprisonment in the arching "round prison" of the sky that shuts in the great globe itself, Ivanhov ends by blowing up the beautiful old house to which he had been welcomed—thus annihilating his residence and himself.

"What is liberty?" inquires a spectator of these libertarian events—Gabriel Gale, Chesterton's mouthpiece. "First and foremost, surely, it is the power of a thing to be itself. In some ways the yellow bird was free in the cage. It was free to be alone. It was free to sing. In the forest its feathers would be torn to pieces and its voice choked for ever. Then I began to think that being oneself, which is liberty, is itself limitation. We are limited by our brains and bodies; and if we break out, we cease to be ourselves, and, perhaps, to be anything."

The Russian psychologist could not abide the necessary conditions of human existence; he must eliminate all limits; he could not endure the "round prison" of the overarching sky. But his alternative was annihilation for himself and his lodging; and he embraced that alternative. He ceased to be anything but fractured atoms. That is the ultimate freedom of the devoted libertarian. If, *per impossible*, our American society should accept the leadership of libertarian ideologues—why, this Republic might end in fractured atoms.

Notwithstanding, there is something to be said for the disintegrated Professor Ivanhov—relatively speaking. With reference to some remarks of mine in a public lecture at Washington, there wrote to me Mr. Marion Montgomery, the Georgia critic and novelist: "The libertarians give me the willies. I prefer the Russian anarchists, who at least have a deeply disturbed moral sensibility (that Dostoevsky makes good use of), to the libertarian anarchists. There is a decadent fervor amongst some of the latter which makes them an unwelcome cross for conservatism to bear."

Just so. The representative libertarian of this era is humorless, intolerant, self-righteous, badly schooled, and dull. At least the old-fangled Russian anarchist was bold, lively, and knew which sex he belonged to.

It is not well-intentioned elderly gentlemen who call themselves libertarians that I reproach here; nor, as I mentioned earlier, those persons who, through misapprehension, lend their names and open their checking accounts to "libertarian" publications and causes and extravagances. Rather, I am exposing the pretensions of the narrow doctrinaires or strutting libertines who have imprisoned themselves within a "libertarian" ideology as confining and as unreal as Marxism—if less persuasive than that fell delusion.

Why are these doctrinaire libertarians, with a few exceptions, such peculiar people—the sort who give healthy folk like Marion Montgomery the willies? Why do genuine conservatives feel an aversion to close association with them? Why is an alliance between conservatives and libertarians inconceivable, except for very temporary purposes? Why, indeed, would any such articles of confederation undo whatever gains conservatives have made in recent years?

I give you a blunt answer to those questions. The libertarians are rejected because they are metaphysically mad. Lunacy repels, and political lunacy especially. I do not mean that they are dangerous: nay, they are repellent merely. They do not endanger our country and our civilization, because they are few, and seem likely to become fewer. (Here I refer, of course, to our home-grown American libertarians, and not to those political sects, among them the Red Brigades of Italy, that have carried libertarian notions to bolder lengths.) There exists no peril that American public policies will be affected in any substantial degree by libertarian arguments; or that a candidate of the tiny Libertarian Party ever will be elected to any public office of significance: the good old causes of Bimetallism, Single Tax, or Prohibition enjoy a more hopeful prospect of success in the closing years of this century than do the programs of Libertarianism. But one does not choose as a partner even a harmless political lunatic.

What do I mean when I say that today's American libertarians are metaphysically mad, and so repellent? Why, the dogmata of libertarianism have been refuted so often, both dialectically and by the hard knocks of experience, that it would be dull work to rehearse here the whole tale of folly. I offer you merely a few of the more conspicuous insufficiencies of libertarianism as a credible moral and political mode of belief. Such differences from the conservatives' understanding of the human condition make inconceivable any coalition of conservatives and libertarians.

First, the great line of division in modern politics, as Eric Voegelin reminds us, is not between totalitarians on the one hand and liberals (or libertarians) on the other: instead, it lies between all those who believe in a transcendent moral order, on the one side, and on the other side all those who mistake our ephemeral existence as individuals for the be-all and end-all. In this discrimination between the sheep and the goats, the libertarians must be classified with the goats—that is, as utilitarians admitting no transcendent sanctions for conduct. In effect, they are converts to Marx's dialectical materialism; so conservatives draw back from them on the first principle of all.

Second, in any tolerable society, order is the first need. Liberty and justice may be established only after order is reasonably secure. But the libertarians give primacy to an abstract Liberty. Conservatives, knowing that "liberty inheres in some sensible object," are aware that freedom may be found only within the framework of a social order, such as the Constitutional order of these United States. In exalting an absolute and indefinable "liberty" at the expense of order, the libertarians imperil the very freedom that they praise.

Third, conservatives disagree with libertarians on the question of what holds civil society together. The libertarians contend—so far as they endure any binding at all—that the nexus of society is self-interest, closely joined to cash payment. But the conservatives declare that society is a community of souls, joining the dead, the living, and those yet unborn; and that it coheres through what Aristotle called friendship and Christians call love of neighbor.

Fourth, libertarians (like anarchists and Marxists) generally believe that human nature is good and beneficent, though damaged by certain social institutions. Conservatives, to the contrary, hold that "in Adam's fall we sinned all": human nature, though compounded of both good and evil, cannot be perfected. Thus the perfection of society is impossible, all human beings being imperfect—and among their vices being violence, fraud, and the thirst for power. The libertarian pursues his illusory way toward a Utopia of individualism—which, the conservative knows, is the path to Avernus.

Fifth, the libertarian asserts that the state is the great oppressor. But the conservative finds that the state is natural and necessary for the fulfillment of human nature and the growth of civilization; it cannot be abolished unless humanity is abolished; it is ordained for our very existence. In Burke's phrases, "He who gave us our nature to be perfected by our virtue, willed also the necessary means of its perfection—He willed therefore the state—He willed its connection with the source and original archetype of all perfection." Without the state, man's condition is poor, nasty, brutish, and short—as Augustine argued, many centuries before Hobbes. The libertarians confound the *state* with *government*; in truth, government is the temporary instrument of the state. But government—as Burke continued—"is a contrivance of human wisdom to provide for human *wants*." Among the more important of these wants is "a sufficient restraint upon their passions. Society requires not only that the passions of individuals should be subjected, but that even in the mass and body, as well as in the individual, the inclinations of men should frequently be thwarted, their will controlled, and their passions brought into subjection. This can be done only *by a power out of themselves*; and not, in the exercise of its function, subject to that will and to those passions which it is its office to bridle and subdue." In short, a primary function of government is restraint; and that is anathema to libertarians, although an article of faith to conservatives.

Sixth, the libertarian fancies that this world is a stage for the ego, with its appetites and self-assertive passions. But the conservative finds himself in a realm of mystery and wonder, where duty, discipline, and sacrifice are required—and where the reward is that love which passeth all understanding. The conservative regards the libertarian as impious, in the sense of the old Roman *pietas*: that is, the libertarian does not respect ancient beliefs and customs, or the natural world, or love of country.

The cosmos of the libertarian is an arid loveless realm, a "round prison." "I am, and none else beside me," says the libertarian. But the conservative replies in the sentence of Marcus Aurelius: "We are made for cooperation, like the hands, like the feet."

These are profound differences; and there exist others. Yet even if conservative and libertarian affirm nothing in common, may they not agree upon a negative? May they not take common ground against totalist ideology and the omnipotent state? The primary function of government, conservatives say, is to keep the peace: by repelling foreign enemies, by administering justice domestically.

When government undertakes objectives far beyond these ends, often government falls into difficulty, not being contrived for the management of the whole of life. Thus far, indeed, conservatives and libertarians hold something in common. But the libertarians, rashly hurrying to the opposite extreme from the welfare state, would deprive government of effective power to conduct the common defense, to restrain the unjust and the passionate, or indeed to carry on a variety of undertakings clearly important to the general welfare. With these failings of the libertarians plain to behold, conservatives are mindful of Edmund Burke's admonition concerning radical reformers: "Men of intemperate mind never can be free. Their passions forge their fetters."

Thus in the nature of things, conservatives and libertarians can conclude no friendly pact. Adversity sometimes makes strange bedfellows, but the recent successes of conservatives disincline them to lie down, lamblike, with the libertarian lions.

By this time, possibly, I have made it sufficiently clear that

I am no libertarian. I venture to suggest that libertarianism, properly understood, is as alien to real American conservatives as is communism. The typical conservative in this country believes that there exists an enduring moral order. He knows that order and justice and freedom are the products of a long and often painful social experience, and that they must be protected from abstract radical assaults. He defends custom, habit, tested institutions that have functioned well. He says that the great virtue in politics is prudence: judging any public measure by its long-run consequences. He is attached to a society of diversity and opportunity, and he is suspicious of any ideology that would rule us by a single abstract principle, whether that principle is "equality" or "liberty" or "social justice" or "national greatness." He recognizes that human nature and society cannot be perfected: politics remains the art of the possible. He adheres to private property and free economic enterprise; he is aware that decent government, repressing violence and fraud, is necessary for the survival of a healthy economy.

What the doctrinaire libertarians offer us is an ideology of universal selfishness—at a time when the country needs more than ever before men and women who stand ready to subordinate their private interests, if need be, to the defense of the Permanent Things. We flawed human creatures are sufficiently selfish already, without being exhorted to pursue selfishness on principle.

Libertarianism as the Philosophy of Moral Freedom

PAUL KURTZ

What is the relationship between liberty and morality? Can one coherently espouse libertarianism, yet deny that it presupposes a moral philosophy? To so argue is contradictory, for the defense of liberty assumes a set of underlying values. But a problem emerges when we attempt to define "libertarianism." It has been taken as an economic doctrine concerned primarily with preserving economic liberty and the free market against the encroachments of government. It has also been used in political philosophy to defend human or natural rights, civil liberties and the open democratic society. Economic and political liberty are indeed central to the libertarian philosophy; they are, however, derivative from an even more fundamental libertarian ideal: the high moral value placed upon individual freedom of choice.

The classical liberal is concerned with expanding the autonomy of persons over their own lives. This means that social restraints placed upon individual choice should be reduced. These are many: large-scale governmental power is a primary threat to individual freedom. Twentieth-century "liberals" under the influence of Marx have abandoned the classic libertarian emphasis on individual freedom in favor of a concern for social welfare. They have sought to extend the paternalistic role of the state in regulating the private sector and fulfilling functions that they believe are not being adequately performed by other social institutions. The welfare liberal believes that it is the duty of society to ameliorate the lot of poor persons and to redistribute wealth—all in the name of a theory of "justice," "fairness," or "equity." The welfare state mentality has unleashed a self-righteous egalitarianism which has undermined the incentives of productive citizens in favor of the disadvantaged. The principle of equality in its extreme form has led reformists beyond advocating equality before the law and equality of opportunity to guaranteeing equality of results. They argue that since not everyone has the same access, social policies must equalize the conditions of opportunity. They would force people to be equal—some more than others—against their will. Libertarians thus have rightly pointed out that doctrines of social equality have been counterproductive, smothering individual initiative, and in Marxist cultures leading to the infamous Gulags of the spirit.

The libertarian agenda is incomplete, however, if it is only concerned with the evils of government. For government is not the only social institution that can unduly restrain human freedom. Powerful economic corporations can erode human freedom, limiting it by defining the conditions of employment, fixing prices, driving out competition, and setting the tone of social life. I am not taking the Marxists' cause here, for I believe that capitalist society is the best guarantee of human freedom. Wherever the state has a monopoly of power, both economic and political freedom soon disappear. A free market and a strong private sector are thus necessary conditions for political freedom. One needs vigorous competition and a pluralistic economy, in which there are diverse centers of economic decision-making.

Libertarians abhor any governmental control of the communications media. They seek a free market of ideas. Yet they must likewise be apprehensive of the *de facto* domination of the media by powerful corporate interests. Much of the mass media—TV, movies, magazines, and newspapers—have been dominated by one point of view: ritualistic liberalism. If the conglomerate control of the publishing industry continues to grow it may tend to push out small publishers and debase the quality of publishing. Western capitalist societies still allow more freedom than others. Thus, I do not agree with Marcuse's pessimistic diagnosis outlined in *One Dimensional Society*. Nevertheless, not all capitalists are libertarians; nor are they necessarily concerned with preserving and extending individual freedom.

The erosion of freedom can also be seen in the growth of large-scale labor unions. The right to work often does not exist in industries where the closed shop operates. There are sound reasons for collective bargaining: the lone individual working for General Motors is no match for the corporation. By entering into a voluntary association with his fellow workers, his ability to bargain collectively more nearly equalizes his economic position. But where unions seek to deny the right to work to those who are not members, they limit choice. No doubt this has been caused by government. But government has been able to legislate the closed shop because of the power of the unions and their members.

This seems also to be the case with regard to religious institutions. Powerful churches have often suppressed unbelievers. In this regard religious institutions may function as oppressively as the state, dictating thought and practice, regulating morality and sexuality, on a *de facto* if not a *de jure* basis. It is always surprising to discover that some conservatives will defend economic liberty, yet readily condone the suppression of religious dissent. Fortunately, American society has had a proliferation of religious denominations and as a result has developed a truce based on the principles of ecumenism. Given the fact of opposing sects all should have a place in the sun. In some areas—fundamentalism in the South or Roman Catholicism in the North—freedom of conscience in religion and morality are still suspect. There is hardly room left for the secular humanist, free thinker, or village atheist in a society dominated by religious tradition. The religious liberal thus defends the separation of church and state and liberty of conscience. Yet conformist pressures seek to impose sanctions on those who violate the prevailing religious conventions.

Perhaps the most encouraging development on the freedom agenda in the past two decades has been the growth of moral libertarianism. The moral premise is familiar: individuals should have the right to satisfy their tastes, cultivate their values, and develop their life styles as they see fit, so long as they do not impose their values on others or prevent them from exercising theirs.

Moral libertarianism has made considerable progress in democratic societies. There has been a noticeable lessening of censorship in the arts, TV, movies, the theater, and magazine and book publishing. Liberty of expression has been extended far beyond what was imagined only a generation ago—but it has led to the growth of the pornography industry. In sexual morality, there has been a loosening of traditional restrictions: divorce has been made easier and is now widespread; laws regulating sexual practices have been repealed; and the belief that two or more consenting adults should have the right to pursue their sexual proclivities without social or legal interference is now widely accepted by a significant sector of the community. This has led in part to the "Gay Liberation" movement. Similar changes have occurred in regard to women, who demand that they be treated as persons capable of choosing their own destinies. Permissive attitudes have also developed concerning drugs. If the state permits alcohol and cigarettes, why not marijuana? Today marijuana is as common in some circles as Coca-Cola, and regrettably so are cocaine and heroin.

In one sense these new freedoms—though they have a liberating effect against stultifying customs—have gone too far. Although one may in principle agree that individuals ought to be allowed to do their own thing, in practice this may lead to a breakdown of civilized conduct, indiscriminate promiscuity, violence, drugs, and a lack of moral virtue and excellence. Many college graduates, in particular, have betrayed the hope and promise placed in them: they are the products of broken homes and a narcissistic morality gone astray. Their rejection of the work ethic is widespread. Living off the generosity of relatives, friends, or social welfare, many have abandoned self-reliance and follow instead subjectivistic self-indulgence. How can one simply defend moral liberty and ignore the loss of virtue? This question is not just theoretical, but has practical import for our society. In mass consumer-oriented society, products are manufactured and sold and tastes conditioned without any regard for their moral worth. The immediacies of enjoyment are taken as ends-in-themselves, divorced from the hard work and effort necessary to achieve them. The quality of life has given way to the banalities.

The above is the indictment that one hears today against the libertarian society. While overstated, it nonetheless has an element of truth. If a choice were to be made between a free society and a repressive one, libertarians would opt for the former, even though they recognize that unfortunate byproducts may have to be suffered. Moreover, the only way for some to learn to appreciate responsible freedom may be to experience the consequences of their mistakes. Nevertheless, at times liberty surely may lead to license when it should be accompanied by virtue. Is the breakdown of the moral order due to the excessive moral freedom that we have enjoyed? May it be attributed to the decline in religious faith and the growth of secular humanism and libertarianism? Is it the case that morality can prevail only if it is guided by religion?

It is not evident that religious societies are any more

moral than non-religious ones. It may be true that outward displays of sexual conduct and other "immoral" practices are often prohibited in repressive religious communities. Yet they may be masking a hypocritical double standard. Religious societies may be insensitive to other forms of injustice. They may seek to impose order, hierarchy and the status quo on those who resist it. But more decisively, a libertarian conception of the moral life which has a secular foundation is different from a religious-theistic one. It is not obedience to a prescribed moral code that is the mark of the moral person, but the flowering of the free personality.

The libertarian in ethics maintains as his first principle the autonomy of moral choice. This means the independence of the ethical judgment: that is, ethical values and principles are not to be deduced *a priori* from absolute rules, but grow out of moral inquiry. Ethical choice requires a sensitivity to moral dilemmas, a willingness to grapple with conflicts in values and principles, rights and duties, as they are confronted in actual life. Authoritarian and legalistic systems of ethics are not based on final or fixed standards. Many traditional religious systems may seek to indoctrinate by fiat a set of norms to guarantee stability and regularity of conduct and inhibit sinful behavior. A religious code such as embodied in the Ten Commandments, the Koran, or the Sermon on the Mount may be supported by the authority of clergy and tradition. It may act as a regulative force, guarding against "defiant," "anomic," or "amoral" behavior. But in what sense are these systems moral? There are traditionalist libertarians in the economic sphere who insist that liberty needs to be supported by religious strictures. They justify religious-moral repression for channeling conduct along approved lines.

A moral libertarian, by way of contrast, rejects authoritarianism in the moral domain as much as he does political statism or economic regulation. Yet he is faced with a profound dilemma. For even if individuals were suddenly released from all restrictions—political, social, moral and traditional—what would ensue? Would they be, as the romantic anarchist hopes, noble, beneficent, sympathetic in their relations to other individuals? Would they be temperate and rational in their inner personal lives? Would their choices be truly autonomous and issue from reflective deliberation?

Regrettably, to emancipate unprepared individuals from all social restraints may indeed result in license. Autonomous choice is not genuine unless individuals are first nurtured to appreciate and handle it. Perhaps the familiar distinction between two kinds of freedom needs to be restated: (1) freedom from restraint is not the same as (2) the developed freedom of a person to realize his potentialities. But there is still another dimension: (3) the full autonomy of choice which can only occur in a developed personality.

Some theists attempt to impose authoritarian structures from without by establishing rules of conduct and instilling them in the young, offering no rhyme or reason other than God's commandments. These homilies often do not take hold, for they do not issue from a person's felt life-world. Although they may erect defenses against temptation and immorality, they can often be weakened and may collapse.

Basically irrational, they do not serve the individual in a changing social world in which new challenges are constantly being presented to him. If they are overthrown, what can the libertarian offer in their place?

The solution to the problem seems to me to be clear: libertarianism in its full sense, i.e., the development of autonomous individuals capable of free choice, is not possible unless certain antecedent conditions are fulfilled. A program of moral education and growth is necessary to instill virtue in the young—not blind obedience to rules, but the ability for conscious reflective choice. The Thrasymachian man, the absolute tyrant, as Plato long ago observed, is prey to every lust and passion, every temptation of power and ambition. He is buffeted by random irrational drives from within, and amoral power conflicts from without. The truly free individual is one whose choices in some sense emanate from a harmonious personality, one with some developed character, a set of dispositional traits, capable of a deliberate process of reasoned decision-making.

This is the message of the great philosophic tradition from Socrates and Aristotle to Spinoza, Mill and Dewey: that rationality and virtue are the source of freedom and emancipation from bondage. And if so, to grant freedom without preparation to a child or adolescent, a savage or despot incapable of reflective choice or mature judgment, unrestrained by seasoned dispositions, is hardly a test of his freedom, for he may be at the mercy of impulses.

Accordingly, freedom makes no sense and it is literally wasted unless it is first nourished in the soil of moral growth, where it can be watered and fed. It is as if democracy were suddenly imposed on a people unready for it, or for which it was alien. It can only function effectively where there are values of tolerance, respect for the views of others, a willingness to negotiate and compromise, and a sense of civic virtue and responsibility. Similarly, true freedom for the individual presupposes the concomitant emergence of moral development. It presumes moral education.

What kind of education and by whom and for what ends? These are important questions. Education is a social process. It goes on constantly—in the family, the churches, the schools, business organizations, the media, in the greater society. It is not the sole responsibility of the state to see that it is done, for that may convert it into a form of mere indoctrination. By education, I mean the Greek form: self-actualization. We need to educate individuals so that they can realize their talents, intellectual, aesthetic, physical. And part of moral education is the developing capacity for self-mastery and control. It also involves the maturation of appreciation and sensitivity for the needs of other human beings. In other words, moral education is training in responsibility: first, towards one's self, one's long-range self-interest in the world, how to cope with and solve problems that emerge in the environment; and second, towards others, some altruistic concern for other human beings, an ability to share life's experiences, to help and be helped, to cooperate with others.

Kohlberg and Piaget have written at length about what they consider to be the stages of moral growth. One need not accept the precise stage theory as presented: from anticipation of reward and punishment, or conformity to social expectations, as motives of moral behavior, to considerations of utility, or the development of a sense of justice, as higher stages of moral growth. Nevertheless, one should surely recognize that there is a process of moral development, for there is a clear difference between the autistic, self-centered individual—some self-interest is an important component of a realistic ethics—and the person able to relate to others under conditions of mutual respect and cooperation. One should more readily be willing to entrust freedom to the latter person, and may—not without cause—be apprehensive about entrusting it to the former. Mill himself recognized that there is an important distinction between the "lower" and "higher" pleasures; the biological pleasures differ in kind from the aesthetic, intellectual and moral pleasures of a developing human being. As a libertarian he was disturbed by the possible abuse of the hedonic criterion and insisted that pleasures differ on a qualitative scale.

To argue, as I have, that a philosophy of liberty most appropriately should involve a theory of virtue does not imply that we should deny freedom to those who are incapable of using it in the fully developed sense. Nor should the government or any self-appointed group set itself up as the arbiter of human freedom. One may consistently believe in a free society, yet also recognize that we have a double obligation: to grant freedom to individuals but also to encourage them to acquire a taste and capacity for growth and autonomy. In this latter regard the best way of doing so is not by dictate, but by means of education and persuasion. Because we tolerate diversity does not mean that we necessarily approve of every style of life, however bizarre or offensive, that has been adopted. We need constantly to keep alive the art of criticism and moral suasion. Liberty does not imply permissiveness. It needs to be accompanied by an ethic which highlights the virtues of the mature personality. This includes *wisdom* (some capacity for intelligent reflective choice), *prudence* and *moderation* (some concern for one's long-range good), and *responsibility* (a genuine interest in the needs of others). Without virtue the person freed from restraint may indeed by transformed into a moral monster.

Philosophers of ethics have consistently maintained that in the last analysis the method of intelligence in an ordered personality is the most reliable guide for moral choice. What we ought to do is a function of a deliberative process wherein we examine alternatives, means, and consequences, and after a comparative analysis make a choice that we consider to be the most suitable in the situation. One of the tasks of moral education is to develop persons who are capable of engaging in moral inquiry.

This will not do, we are reminded by criticism of moral libertarianism, particularly those of a non-secularist bent. Merely to have an autonomous individual is no guarantee that he will behave morally toward himself or others. We cannot educate men to be virtuous, we are told, without the authority of divine sanction. If the only guide is utilitarian ends whether for the individual or the social good, then anything is possible and all things may be permissible. The critics of secular humanism and libertarianism also attack the effort now under way to develop moral education and values clarification in the schools. They believe that this is a "secular religion" which will only further undermine the moral standards of society.

Now it is true that many or most libertarians have emphasized utilitarian considerations in the decision-making process. Moral principles are held to be largely instrumental in the fulfillment of ends of values. The hedonic calculus judges actions by whether they maximize pleasure or happiness in the individual and society. Most libertarians have been relativists, situationalists and naturalists. Such ethical theories have lacked a well-grounded theory of moral duty and obligation. In my view, however, this need not be the case. Libertarianism indeed is incomplete as a moral philosophy and remains seriously in need of repair unless it is willing to modify its ethical system so that it can introduce deontological considerations.

What I have in mind here is the recognition that there are general ethical principles that ought to prevail in human relationships. These are grounded in human experience, and have been tested in the crucible of history. Moral principles, in my judgment, are not simply an expression of subjective taste or caprice, but may have some empirical foundation. They are amenable to objective criticism. The human decencies are readily recognized by most human societies: we ought to tell the truth, be sincere, honest, and deal fairly with others; we ought to be cooperative, kind, considerate, thoughtful, helpful; we ought not to waste our patrimony needlessly; we ought not to misuse others, be arrogant and unforgiving; we ought not to inflict pain needlessly or cruelly, not be excessively vindictive; we ought to have friends, not simply acquaintances; we ought to seek justice and be beneficent.

This list of ethical principles is embodied in the proverbial truths discovered in human affairs. Many or most—but surely not all—are transcultural. They are general guides to conduct not universal or absolute, since exceptions can be made to them on occasion. Nor are they intuitive or self-evident; if they are tested, it is by their observable consequences in conduct. They have some foundation in our sense of reason; and they may be given some strength in our motivation, and be enhanced by emotion and feeling. They involve both our attitudes and beliefs. They are *prima facie*, for they would seem to express general rules of conduct, which people come to recognize and respect as binding. How they apply and to what extent depends on the context. Sometimes one or more ethical principles may conflict. They may conflict with our cherished values. Moral deliberation is usually difficult, and often we must choose between the lesser of two evils; there may be a clash between two goods or two rights, both of which we cannot have.

These ethical principles embody moral truths. We may learn from practical experience that they cannot be easily violated without unfortunate consequences. They may be certified on their own level without being derived or deduced from questionable antecedent theological or metaphysical assumptions. They have a kind of authenticity in human experience.

Thus one may respond to the critics of moral libertarianism in the following manner:

> (1) Moral conduct is possible without belief in God, or benefit of religion or clergy. (Believers are not more moral than unbelievers.)
> (2) Reasonable moral choices can be made and moral

knowledge discovered in the process of human living
and experience.
(3) Accordingly, there can be an intelligent basis for
moral obligations and responsibility.

Thus one can be a moral libertarian and a secularist
without being a libertine or degenerate, and one may
display the marks of nobility and excellence as part of the
good life (as exemplified in the philosophies of Aristotle
and Spinoza). One may also, in this post-Freudian age, live
a significant moral life which contains passion and reason,
enjoyment and happiness, creativity and responsibility.

Freedom is not simply a claim to be made against society
or a demand to be left alone, but, in the sense of a human
nature that is seeking improvement, is a capacity to be
earned and achieved. Freedom is not to be experienced
indiscriminately nor squandered stupidly. It is an art to be
cultivated and nourished intelligently. The intemperate
person is neither autonomous nor civilized in regard to
himself nor in his relations with others. Liberty and moral
development go hand in hand; the one can enhance the
other. There is no complete freedom until there is the
developed capacity for maturity in judgment and action.
There can be no fully autonomous person unless there is
realized growth.

Various forms of libertarianism surely can be defended
independently of a secular focus. One can be an economic
libertarian or civil libertarian, a born again Christian,
Buddhist monk, practicing Jew, devout Hindu or Roman
Catholic. We should not insist that secular libertarianism
is the only basis for the moral life. I happen to believe that
it is the one most in accord with the realities of nature and

the promise of individual attainment. In a pluralistic society, those who wish to believe in God or to base their morality on religious faith should be perfectly free to do so. For many moderns, however, God is dead; indeed, He never lived. But to be committed to the secular city does not mean that morality is dead or without moorings. Ethics is a vital dimension of the human condition and a recognition of the ethical life has deep roots within Western philosophy antecedent even to the Judeo-Christian tradition. The current attack on secular morality is a display of philistine ignorance about the origins of Western civilization in Hellenic culture and its historic philosophic development. It is an attack on the philosophic life itself.

The charges against moral libertarianism are thus unfounded. Those who now oppose it cannot tolerate moral freedom nor can they stand to see other individuals suffer or enjoy life as they choose. But who are they to seek to impose their values on others? The fact that they assume a mantle of divine sanction for their views makes them no more authoritative. Moreover, they fail to appreciate the fact that a moral person is not one who obeys a moral code out of fear or faith but who is motivated to behave morally out of a sense of moral awareness and conviction. The exemplar for the moral libertarian is the free person, capable of choice, who has achieved some measure of moral growth. He is the master of his own fate, responsible for his own career and destiny.

The free person is unlike the obedient servant or slave who follows a moral code simply because it is commanded by authority or tradition. He is independent, resourceful, has confidence in his powers, and faith that he can lead the good life. Moreover, he can enter into dignified relationships of trust and sincerity with his fellow human beings. He can live a constructive, productive, and responsible life. The moral philosophy of libertarian humanism is thus worthy of admiration. It needs no apology against those who seek to demean or denigrate its excellence or virtue. In a sense it is the highest expression of moral virtue: a tribute to the indomitable creative spirit of human achievement and personality.

Libertarianism as the Philosophy of Moral Freedom: A Response

Edward B. McLean

If there is no determinant and proper object toward which liberty is to be directed, then any object for which it is employed must be considered equally valuable. If, however, one concludes that all human acts are not equally valued, and that some acts are to be preferred over others which are to be disallowed, then one must search for those criteria by which such valuations are to be made. Prof. Kurtz appeals to human experience and man's history. These are frail reeds on which to construct a plea that liberty is desirable. Man's history and experience, although it shows greatness and goodness, also reveals baseness and evil of such a magnitude and scope that one trembles at the prospect that man might rely on certain sets of experience and history to fashion the purposes for which his liberty will be used. More important is the fact that Prof. Kurtz's prescription contains no basis on which to condemn evil developments, other than hortatory statements to the effect that other choices are preferable. There is no internal standard derivable from a concept of human liberty—

standing alone—to measure "good" acts and "bad" acts. Indeed, such an argument can provide justification only for acts generally.

Any merit liberty has is derivative from a presumed transcendent order of goodness against which the value of individual acts can be measured. It is true, as Prof. Kurtz states, that human liberty can be used for good, but this statement alone is no demonstration of that as a necessary result. Individual acts exercised for objects desired by the actor are not condemnable by others except by reference to a standard not fashioned by the actors, and a series of actions joined in by others, in a concentrated effort to do evil to others, are not condemnable by others except by reference to a standard not fashioned by those actors; that is, appeal must be made to a transcendent standard which identifies certain actions as evil and shows that converse actions are good. Prof. Kurtz could not argue his thesis as effectively as he does, unless he borrowed and utilized language that is the product and result of Judeo-Christian beliefs. Without language derived from these beliefs his article could not be written so that its purpose could be understood by the reader. The Judeo-Christian basis for Western liberty honors and treasures liberty. Indeed— except for certain aberrations of Christian doctrine—the coming to God is the highest expression of free will, and acts in conformity with God's ordinances are acts of free will. All constructive notions of liberty are infused with the predicates of Christian faith and cannot be sustained without their explicit or implicit guidance.

Central to Prof. Kurtz's thoughts on liberty, as we have noted, is his endorsement of the belief that men should keep their word. Certainly the market mechanism could not function well without such a notion. At its root such an injunction is not sustainable as an absolute; that is, it is perfectly capable of qualification and condition, depending on the intent, desire, and object of the one who gave his word. Arguing from a standpoint of utility one could conceivably maintain that forcing people to keep their word results cumulatively in more frequent and extensive benefits. Such an argument, however, must further agree that if this were not the case then there would exist no compelling reason for men to keep their word. Even more vexing is the realization that while the argument for supporting this injunction might be predicated on its utility, it loses its force of persuasion when an individual does not apply it to his individual case. The point is that such an injunction is suspendable and revocable when measured by utility, majority preferences, or individual aspirations. When such an injunction is predicated on a transcendental standard that is neither suspendable nor revocable in any justifiable sense for any reason, whether it is utility, majority preference, or individual desire, then it becomes a genuine argument for compelling one to keep his word. When it is accepted that the standard of morality exists above men, then it is a defensible, workable, and moral principle which is not contextual or relational; it is, rather, an absolute to be honored by all. Such a standard provides a sustainable and defensible framework within which expectations can be protected, interactions encouraged, and measures of the proper use of liberty made.

Prof. Kurtz's assumption that such a value is derivable and sustainable from human experiences and history is an error—witness the abrogation of all forms of contract relations entered into by Jews in Germany which were or could be abrogated on a moment's notice by action of the German government. Without reference to a transcendental standard that provides an unchangeable moral basis for the argument that men should keep their word, one can legitimately suspend such a notion under any given set of circumstances. Thus, paradoxically, Prof. Kurtz's argument leads necessarily to justification of power as the only measure of the value of keeping one's word, since if it is not a moral obligation it can only be an obligation secured by force. Certainly this is not the intended consequence suggested, but it inevitably flows from the argument of a self-defining concept of liberty. For those who profited from breaking agreements with Jews, the concepts of efficiency, propriety, and utility were met. What could not be met, and what is therefore critical to any defense of the idea of keeping one's word, is the acceptance, as true, of a transcendent concept of morality which is not derived from human experience and history, but transcends both in time and space. It is from these religiously determined values that coherence and meaning of concepts, such as keeping one's word, are derived. The acceptance of and belief in such transcendent values can be the only logical source from which the standard Prof. Kurtz applauds can be derived—they are not and cannot be derived from the concept of liberty standing alone and considered unrelated to transcendent values.

In summarizing his argument, Prof. Kurtz makes three assertions of how and why moral libertarianism is a defensible concept. He asserts:

(1) Moral conduct is possible without belief in God, or benefit of religion or clergy. (Believers are not more moral than unbelievers.)(200)

This statement contains only one-half of its necessary content. In order for this statement to be complete it must go on to recognize that immoral conduct is never justifiable under Christian religion, and even though a believer or a clergyman may act immorally, he may never do so justifiably within the canons of the faith. Thus, in the context of a religious belief, standards of morality are transcendent ones which condemn certain conduct as immoral regardless of time or place or motive. Prof. Kurtz's arguments for libertarianism as moral philosophy cannot do this, for each individual—in the exercise of his liberty—must ultimately provide his own measure and his own standard. Since there is no transcendent standard to judge human acts in this scheme, there is no relevance in the concept of moral conduct, and the only truth in such a conclusion is that moral conduct is possible—but is neither necessary nor required. Human conduct which is "moral," therefore, is a hope, not a standard.

Prof. Kurtz argues:

(2) Reasonable moral choices can be made and moral knowledge discovered in the process of human living and experience. (200-201)

Again, he presents only half the argument, for absent a set of transcendental values, unreasonable moral choices can be made and immoral "knowledge" discovered or perpetuated. Contextually, Mussolini's fascism advances what it identifies as reasonable moral choices and speaks endlessly of the discovery of moral knowledge embodied in the wisdom of the state. How can this be disproved except by reference to a transcendental set of beliefs that posit as fundamental and unalterable the dignity and worth of all men as *individuals*, and which considers all acts, however disguised by rhetoric of casuistry or compelled by the force of events, which deny to individual men as individual men their dignity and their value, as reprehensible and immoral.

Finally, he says:

> (3) Accordingly [in light of his two preceding half statements], there can be an intelligent basis for moral obligations and responsibility. (201)

One must comment on the offensiveness of this statement. In the context in which it is made, this statement suggests that anyone who is not a "moral libertarian" cannot be guided by intelligence. Such a casual rejection of the profound search for truth in the writing of St. Thomas Aquinas, to mention only one of the great Christian philosophers, is at best a gratuitous insult. St. Thomas was aware that man's reason could lead him to rational conduct in conformance with natural law, but that this is not sufficient for man given his nature and purpose, nor sufficient to prevent his lapse into barbarism and cruelty. Prof. Kurtz's argument can in no way provide a secure basis against a society of cruelty which is derivable exclusively from history and experience. His case for an "intelligent basis" on which to build moral obligation could justify Marxist or Fascist regimes as well as liberal democratic societies, for as he says, "The exemplar for the moral libertarian is the free person, capable of choice, who has achieved some measure of moral growth."(202) Is this not the "free person" of whom Mussolini writes who understands that "true" freedom is to be found in submission to the Fascist state, or the Marxist who recognizes that all "bourgeois notions of freedom" are not really such, for true freedom is to be found in the final transition to a Communist Utopia? It is evident that this is not in the least what Prof. Kurtz seeks or wants but in rejecting the central, determinative, and necessary role of religion from his argument he cannot and does not provide any effective barrier—intellectual or moral—to such developments.

One can conclude that Prof. Kurtz must accept the idea which is discussed in *The Brothers Karamazov* that without God, all things are lawful. To be sure, one avenue from this denial of God could lead to a society of civility and relative goodness, but the other avenue leads to evil and barbarism. One would hope that libertarian philosophers would accept the fact that their notions have merit only in relation to the religious basis of Western civilization, and that the liberty they seek is valuable so long as the ends toward which it is directed are derived from transcendent truths and values which are God's and not man's.

**Page references in notation are to Professor Kurtz's essay.

Freedom and Virtue: Allies or Antagonists?

Doug Bandow

Both freedom and virtue are under assault today. The attack on economic and political freedom is obvious enough. Government takes and spends roughly half of the nation's income. Regulation further extends the power of the state in virtually every area—how one can use one's property, what occupation one can enter, who one can hire, what terms one can offer to prospective employees, with which countries one can trade. Increasing numbers of important, personal decisions are ultimately up to some functionary somewhere, rather than the average citizen.

The problem only got worse during the 1980s despite the election of avowedly conservative presidents. Spending and regulation rose particularly dramatically during the Bush administration. Alas, government is likely to expand even more quickly over the next several years.

Virtue, too, seems to be losing ground daily. Evidence of moral decline was evident enough in the last presidential election. Bill Clinton's widely reported promiscuous adul-

tery makes a mockery of his church attendance; his eva-
sions and lies regarding his draft avoidance suggest that his
commitment to the truth is weak at best. George Bush,
while apparently leading a more exemplary personal life,
thought nothing of making a promise on taxes that he
never intended to keep and appears to have dissembled
badly regarding his knowledge of the Iran-Contra affair.
The shamelessness and viciousness of his attacks on his
opponent in the 1992 campaign were also not the stuff of
which virtue is made.

Things are scarcely better elsewhere in society. Promiscuity is not just a twentysomething phenomenon; even
many preteens are sexually active. Illegitimacy rates continue to rise not only in the inner city but also in middle
class America. Dishonesty and theft are the rage: the entire
political system is geared to facilitate special interest looting
of the taxpayers. Employees as well as customers shop-
lift—everywhere. Some years ago a university band distinguished itself by stealing more than $30,000 worth of
merchandise while visiting Japan. Business, too, suffers
from a corrupt core, as was demonstrated by Ivan Boesky
and his ilk in the 1980s.

Some elements of our society have attacked both freedom
and virtue. Much of the left, for instance, believes in
"choice" if it means moral relativism and escape from
responsibility, but abhors "choice" if it means private
individuals making informed decisions about their children, kids' educations, jobs, and other aspects of their lives.

Alas, some advocates of liberty and virtue have compounded the problem by unnecessarily setting the two against each other. A number of members of the more "libertarian" right dismiss virtue as a matter of concern, while some more traditional conservatives want the state to circumscribe individual freedom to promote "morality." Both of these groups see freedom and virtue as frequent antagonists, if not permanent opponents. At the very least, they suggest, you cannot maximize both of them, but, instead, have to choose which to promote and which to restrict.

However, it is a mistake to assume that one must be sacrificed for the other. Freedom and virtue are related, but are complementary. That is, liberty—the right to exercise choice, free from coercive state regulation—is a necessary precondition for virtue. And virtue is ultimately necessary for the survival of liberty.

Virtue cannot exist without freedom, without the right to make moral choices. By virtue I mean the dictionary definition: moral excellence, goodness, righteousness. Coerced acts of conformity with some moral norm, however good, do not represent virtue; rather, the compliance with that norm must be voluntary.

There are times, of course, when coercion is absolutely necessary—most importantly, to protect the rights of others by enforcing an *inter*-personal moral code governing the relations of one to another. The criminal law is an obvious example, as is the enforcement of contracts and property rights. But is coercion justified to promote virtue, that is, to impose a standard of *intra*-personal morality? At stake are some of the most controversial issues: drug use, pornography, homosexuality, and the like. All of these activities have some social impact and some people argue that it is precisely this impact that justifies state intervention. More powerful, however, is the contrary case against intervention—that most of the ill consequences, such as drug-related crime, are primarily a product of legal prohibition rather than the activity itself. If, in fact, government regulation makes the social problems worse, then the only justification for intervention is to promote virtue.

Our nation's moral tone is not good; America does not seem to be a particularly virtuous place. And the moral environment seems to have gotten worse in recent years, though, of course, one should have no illusions that a perfect age every existed. Still, if things have gotten worse, one has to ask: is that because we have become more free, and would becoming less free make America more virtuous?

The answers to both questions, I think, are no.

The natural human condition, certainly in Christian theology, and in historical experience, too, is not one of virtue. "There is no one righteous, not even one," Paul wrote in his letter to the Roman church, citing the Psalms (Rom. 3:10). This explains the necessity of a transcendent plan of redemption.

But societies can be more or less virtuous. Did ours become less so *because* government no longer tried so hard to mold souls? Blaming moral shifts on legal changes mistakes correlation for causation. In fact, America's one-time cultural consensus eroded even during an era of strict laws against homosexuality, pornography, and even fornication. Only cracks in this consensus led to changes in the law. In short, as more people viewed sexual mores as a matter of taste rather than a question of right or wrong, the moral underpinnings of the law collapsed, followed by the laws. Only a renewed consensus could allow the re-establishment of the laws.

But the government is not a particularly good teacher of virtue. The state tends to be good at simple, blunt tasks, like killing and jailing people. It has been far less successful at reshaping individual consciences. Even if one could pass the laws without changing America's current moral ethic, the result would not be a more virtuous nation. True, there might be fewer overt acts of immorality. But there would be no change in people's hearts. Forcibly preventing people from victimizing themselves does not automatically make them more virtuous, righteous, or good. As Christ instructed his listeners, "Anyone who looks at a woman lustfully has already committed adultery with her in his heart" (Mt. 5:28). A country full of people lusting in their hearts who don't consummate the lust out of fear of arrest is scarcely better than one full of people acting on their sinful whims. It is, in short, one thing to improve appearances, but quite another to improve society's moral core. And God, Jeremiah tells us, looks at the heart (Jer. 17:10).

Indeed, attempting to forcibly make people virtuous would make society itself less virtuous in three important ways. First, individuals would lose the opportunity to exercise virtue. They would not face the same set of temptations and be forced to choose between good and evil. This approach might thereby make their lives easier—it might also make them less vulnerable to a number of diseases. But they would not be more virtuous and society would suffer as a result. In this dilemma we see the paradox of Christianity: a God of love creates man and provides a means for his redemption, but allows him to choose to do evil. While true Christian liberty means freedom from sin, it seems to be tied to a more common form of freedom, the opportunity to choose whether to respond to God's grace.

Second, to vest government with primary responsibility for promoting virtue shortchanges other institutions, or "governments" in Puritan thought, like the family and church, sapping their vitality. Private social institutions find it easier to lean on the power of coercion than to lead by example, persuade, and solve other problems. Moreover, the law is better at driving immorality underground than eliminating it. As a result, moral problems seem less acute and we are less uncomfortable; we are therefore less likely to work as hard to promote virtue.

Third, making government a moral enforcer encourages abuse by majorities or influential minorities that gain power. If one thing is certain in life, it is that man is sinful. "There is no one righteous, not even one" states a biblical passage that bears repeating. The effect of sin is magnified by the possession and exercise of coercive power. Its possessors can, of course, do good, but history suggests that they are far more likely to do harm. Even in our democratic system majorities are as ready to enact their personal predilections—okaying the use of such dangerous substances as alcohol and tobacco while outlawing marijuana—as uphold real morality.

And as America's traditional Judeo-Christian consensus crumbles we are more likely to see government promoting alternative moral views—teaching that gay unions are normal, and so on. This is possible only if government is given the authority to coercively mold souls in order to "promote virtue." Despite the best intentions of advocates of statecraft as soulcraft, government is far more likely to end up enshrining immorality as morality. All told, an unfree society is not likely to be a virtuous one.

The fact that government can do little to help does not mean that there is nothing it should do. We would all be better off if public officials adopted as their maxim, "First, do no harm." Although the community-wide moral break-down most evident in the inner city has many causes, government policy has exacerbated the problem. Welfare, for instance, has made illegitimacy and family break-up financially feasible and often profitable. The ever-worsening drug war has robbed urban residents of hope and created well-funded criminal gangs that offer male role models and wealth to fatherless, ill-educated ghetto youth. Economic restrictions, such as the minimum wage and occupational licensing, have made it difficult for residents to find even ill-paid legal work. Monopoly government schools don't train inner city residents for remunerative, satisfying employment even if it existed. Finally, housing regulations—rent control, zoning, and the like—have helped trap the poor in slums. The synergistic impact of all these factors operating together has been devastating.

Governments also punish both marriage and thrift through their tax policies. The state has spent years attempting to expunge not only churches but also religious values from the public square: localities war against religion through everything from zoning restrictions to private school regulations. Indeed, government at all levels has proved itself to be the greatest of imperialists, constantly expanding—all the while displacing or regulating private activities.

Beyond doing no harm, public institutions can perform an educative role, but the moral discourse needs to be carried on at the broadest level of consensus possible. It is unreasonable, for instance, to expect a state government to launch a crusade against homosexuality, as Proposition 9 would have directed the state of Oregon. Not only are gays taxpayers, but there seems little reason to single them out while ignoring adulterers and fornicators, for instance. The broader issue, with greater social consequences, is promiscuity. Similarly, there is general agreement from across the philosophical spectrum that teens should not be having children: therefore abstinence can be promoted in public schools for reasons other than adherence to traditional Jewish and Christian moral teachings.

However, advocates of virtue must be careful in using the state in even this modest fashion lest they abdicate their own essential roles in the educative process. Moreover, while the government may help buttress private instruction, it remains a very imperfect tool and subject to misuse by officials and special interest groups with their own, usually very political, agendas. Indeed, in the end, what goes around tends to come around. Once advocates of virtue use the state to politicize the process, they lose their strongest argument, on principle, for preventing other forces from using government for immoral ends.

Nevertheless, freedom is not enough. While liberty is the highest political goal, it is not life's highest objective. Moreover, while a liberal, in the classical sense, economic and political system is the best one available, it will operate even better if nestled in a virtuous social environment.

For instance, a market system will function more effectively if people are honest and voluntarily fulfill their contracts. People who believe in working hard, exercising thrift, and observing temperance will be more productive. Economic life will function more smoothly if employers treat their workers fairly. Fewer social problems will emerge if families, churches, and communities organize to forestall them in the first place. Greater personal responsibility will reduce welfare expenditures and tort litigation. And so on. A lush lawn of a compassionate, cooperative, and virtuous society will make it harder for weeds of government encroachment to flourish.

Thus, advocates of a minimal state need to be concerned about both liberty and virtue. Freedom is important both as an end in itself and as a means of allowing people to exercise virtue. Virtue, too, is critically important in its own right. It also plays a critical role in undergirding a free society. How best can we promote them together? First, as noted earlier, government should do no harm. We need radical changes in policies that today restrict freedom and undermine morality. Second, private mediating institutions, particularly churches and community associations, need to retake their leading role in teaching virtue and meeting social problems. Third, people need to be more willing to tolerate the quirks and failings, even serious virtuous lapses, of their neighbors, so long as such actions have only limited effect on others. The punishment of most sins should be left to God.

Fourth, moral-minded citizens should turn to the state only as a last resort. The issue needs to be important enough to warrant government intervention; the activity involved also needs to have a significant impact on non-consenting parties. And *private alternatives should be clearly inadequate.* For example, religious believers should lead their children in prayer at home rather than foisting that duty onto atheist teachers in the public schools. Opponents of pornography should organize boycotts before demanding the arrest of buyers and sellers. And, perhaps most importantly, vocal supporters of the importance of virtue need to exhibit morality in their own lives before suggesting that government place cops in other people's bedrooms.

Those of us who believe in both a free and virtuous society face serious challenges in the coming years. We need to respond by finding ways to strengthen both, not play them off each other. In the end, neither is likely to survive without the other.

Love versus *Freedom*

FREDERICK D. WILHELMSEN

A tale is told—it is not apocryphal—that when Lenin and Trotsky were drawn up on the outskirts of Moscow in a train after the communist victory, the whole country in ruins and tens of thousands dead and still lying in the fields unburied, Trotsky asked Lenin: "But now are we going to have freedom?" Lenin answered: "Freedom? For what?" In this exchange, I am going to take Lenin's side against Trotsky, although personally I have always found Trotsky to be a more sympathetic figure than Lenin.

Our goal here, as I understand it, is the role of love and liberty within a commonwealth that would embrace both. My opponent is free and I am in love.* Many readers of this exchange are too young to remember the famous debate between L. Brent Bozell and Frank Meyer that worked itself out in the pages of *National Review*. Although the subject

---

*This essay was part of a debate between Frederick Wilhelmsen and Doug Bandow sponsored by the Intercollegiate Studies Institute on the topic: Freedom or Virtue? See previous essay.

was couched in terms of virtue and freedom, the subject in truth was the same facing us today. I am filled with *déjà vu*. Years pass and the applications of philosophical options change but the delineations seem to retain their original lineaments.

Permit me to advance a philosophical proposition, the truth of which is evident to anyone who attends carefully to what he does when he chooses anything freely. Liberty is a function of Love. Choice bears upon means capable of achieving what I love at this moment. My love may be vicious or noble; it may be steady or ephemeral but nobody is free when he loves, in the moment in which he loves. There is an eternity about the act of love even if it lasts for only a minute. When a man says to a woman, "I love you," unless he be a liar bent on conquest, what he intends is eternal. The love may pass but while it lasts it enjoys an everlasting character.

If I were to spend the evening at leisure (I was perhaps free to make this decision but once made it is my love), I would command my intellect to discover the means whereby I might achieve that love. I might determine that I can fulfill my desire by reading a book I have wanted to read for some time; by lounging in my room doing nothing; by going to a motion picture; by playing chess with a friend. Note carefully: None of these is my end, neither reading the book, lounging in my room, playing chess, or anything else. My concrete end is an evening of leisure. As means, no one of them determines me because the others will do the job as well. Not being determined, I determine myself. This self-determination in reference to an end is the essence of free choice. Free choice is an act of the will towards some finality loved, and that act is not determined if there is a multiplicity of ends capable of fulfilling the same goal. Somebody once asked G.K. Chesterton what book he would want—he could only have one—were he exiled on a desert island. Chesterton answered: a manual on how to build a boat. His end would be to get off that bloody island and go home. If the only way to do so was to build a boat, he would build a boat or at least try to build a boat. When only one means emerges as capable of reaching our end, there is no freedom at all. Freedom emerges as a psychological possibility when there is more than one means to a finality, none determining the will but each capable of achieving the goal. Freedom psychologically is always a means, never an end.

From this we can draw the conclusion that no polity under the sun has ever been constructed around freedom as an end. The business is a philosophical and psychological impossibility. We are *not* free with reference to goals we love, and these goals antedate any exercise of liberty on our part. Often classical liberalism and libertarianism have raised the banner of absolute liberty as a political goal. But this cannot be done, try as we may. Love governs liberty. When men try to pull this off, they end in tyranny. Plato's "democratic man" lacks any fixed goal or love. His psyche soon degenerates into being the slave of his passions. If I am not guided from some star without, be that star noble or ignoble, I will be governed from within by the basest of my instincts.

Political freedom in the West was born, teaches Lord Acton, when the subject of existence, the individual person, was institutionalized in the Middle Ages in more than one way. Being a member of a guild, a township, kingdom or empire and Church, man had to choose in case of a conflict between them. Where there is no conflict between means—and means always conflict because the selection of one of them involves the abandonment of the others—there is no liberty, no political freedom. And these choices are always made in the light of some love that moved the man making the choice.

Every polity known to man historically has been knit into being, rendered thereby the polity that it is, by some love annealing into unity and society men who would otherwise be isolated into an anarchy, Hong Kong or Singapore versus the United States or France, let us say. Many years ago I coined the term "public orthodoxy" to describe that to which I refer here: the public orthodoxy consists in those convictions, and our love for them, that stamps upon a society the seal of its very identity, that makes this community to be what it is. This public affirmation of the absolute can be enshrined in a constitution. It does not have to be. It can be discovered in the songs, the art, the style of being surrounding any given society. At bottom this affirmation is always religious because it reflects how men respond to their brush with the absolute. Societies are what they are thanks to what they love, and freedom within such communities, should it flourish, is always in terms of something more profound than liberty: it is love.

If the question before the house is either liberty or love, then I insist that the opposition is false. If the love be a love of virtue then that love englobes liberty because without liberty virtue is always truncated.

If, however, the question is crafted in such fashion that we are asked to elect either love as an end or freedom as an end, we face a sundering sword separating traditionalists from libertarians and quasi-libertarians and, I must add, traditionalists from neo-conservatives. Nests of contradictions swarm into the debate and render it futile at bottom. If by freedom we mean choice, and thus far this is the meaning I am giving to the word, then I think I have demonstrated already that choice can never be an end in itself. Even more: if we were to choose between choosing *and* a good loved and cherished, then some even deeper end must be loved by us that presumably can be fulfilled by one another of these two putative means. But one of them, choice for the sake of choosing, is no end at all and furthermore—even if we could pull off this psychological legerdemain—in what service would this choosing be?

But there is a second and even deeper meaning to the word liberty, a liberty beyond freedom of choice, and this is *liberation* from evil. Although the man whose character is not annealed in the good proper to his nature can occasionally choose to act decently, this act is difficult, rare, and capricious. Virtue—the teaching is Aristotle's—involves a steadying of the will which makes honorable decisions relatively easy. The good man does not have to agonize over whether he will pay what he owes. He just pays out of a nature inclined towards honesty through much experience in being honest. Virtuous life and the love for it is all the more virtuous in the measure of the ease with which we exercise our liberty towards the good.

From these considerations follows the truth that a political order geared toward nourishing the good life and virtue, its love, removes—to the degree possible—the temptation to vice, to wickedness. If we have chosen virtue over vice, then we shore up the weak, strengthen our young, and we outlaw depravity when we have to. Love opposes liberty only when liberty opposes love. The question must shift to the content of love. If conformed to man's good, then liberty is properly put to that lofty service. If the love is opposed to man's good, then liberty is properly repressed by an ordained love—as does the love of a father for his son's good prohibit that boy from losing himself in debauchery. Laws against pornography, public indecency, abnormal behavior, the glorification of greed and gluttony, and finally—abortion, cut down a man's choices but in doing so liberate him, free him from temptation and open him to the good life. We all know the nineteenth century romantic tales about good men who play the piano in brothels. As entertaining as these stories might be (I found one or two of them very amusing), they can scarcely be thought to reflect reality soberly. If you live in filth, you are going to get dirty. Every good polity protects the virtue of its people but, paradoxically, this limitation of the freedom of choice is for the sake of the higher liberation from evil of which I have just spoken.

I sometimes think that men such as my old friend Frank Meyer, now gone to God, thought that we should make it hard for people to be good by permitting every option, no matter how evil, to stalk the streets and tempt the soul. Possibly this extreme exaltation of freedom wants the good life restricted to those few who are strong but who are willing to let the rest of us wallow in sin. I find here a lack of charity. I *am* my brother's keeper! Our weaker brethren and our children, possibly the mass of mankind, are also called to virtue and society is obliged under its command to seek the common good to make it feasible for them to find the good. Every society protects its public orthodoxy or way of life. Censorship is consubstantial with political existence. Liberals usually censor conservatives by silencing them, not publishing them, banishing them from television and other mass media, denying them tenure at universities. But the children of mammon are wiser than the children of light! This effective repression would be normal behavior were it not compounded with the hypocrisy that *they* are the party of liberty. The traditionalist is more honest when he states flatly, as I do here, that some repression and censorship are indispensable for the flowering of good men in the large and by the handful.

The usual skeptical and relativist reply to such reasoning is the customary epistemological negativism. Some of you are thinking it right now! How do you know what is the good to be loved? What if your good not be mine? And all of this goes with the talk today about "values," yours versus mine. And the answer to this is simply to point to the two thousand and more years of Western civilization which have built up slowly a consensus on the nature and content of the natural law, itself a participation in the Divine Law. If the decay caused by publicly and even legally established skepticism denies that tradition, then all standards collapse, and we return to the jungle. Then indeed we choose for the sake of choosing, we raise the banner of total liberty which soon collapses, as Plato taught, in the tyranny of the passions. We are there already.

We cannot walk in the streets of our cities at night. Our

houses and apartments are turned into armed camps. Our children are sexually abused and our women raped with impunity. Half of the American population is armed to the teeth. No man can trust his own shadow. No common belief unites us in anything and as civility becomes a memory, perversion and infanticide are converted into "alternative life styles." Our only hope is the Lock and the Key as Hobbes once put it, keeping out the savagery from beyond. *But we are all free! Are we not?* Into these ruins has collapsed what was once the glory of mankind, Western Christian civilization, "the saving grace of this world," in Belloc's immortal prose. And that grace is now gone because rejected in the name of a false understanding of liberty.

Notes on Contributors

M. Morton Auerbach was professor of Political Science at the University of California at Northridge. He is the author of *The Conservative Illusion.*

Doug Bandow is a Senior Fellow at the Cato Institute and the author of *Beyond Good Intentions: A Biblical View of Politics.*

Walter Berns has taught at Yale, Cornell, Georgetown, and the University of Toronto. He is John M. Olin Distinguished Scholar in Constitutional and Legal Studies at the American Enterprise Institute. Among his works is *The First Amendment and the Future of American Democracy.*

L. Brent Bozell (1925-1997) was a senior editor of *National Review* and later founded *Triumph*, a conservative Catholic journal. Among his works is *The Warren Revolution: Reflections on the Consensus Society.*

George W. Carey is Professor of Government at Georgetown University. He is the author and editor of several works including *In Defense of the Constitution.* He is also editor of *The Political Science Reviewer*, an annual review of leading works in political science and related disciplines.

John P. East (1931-1986) was a Professor of Political Science at East Carolina University. He was elected to the United States Senate from North Carolina in 1980 and served in that capacity until his death. He authored *The American Conservative Movement*.

M. Stanton Evans is the director of the National Journalism Center in Washington, D.C. and former editor of the *Indianapolis News*. His most recent work is *The Theme Is Freedom: Religion, Politics, and the American Tradition*.

John Hospers was Professor of Philosophy at the University of Southern California and the first Libertarian Party candidate for president in 1972. He is the author of *Libertarianism, Understanding the Arts,* and *Introduction to Philosophical Analysis*.

Russell Kirk (1918-1994) was one of this century's foremost men of letters. He was the founder of the conservative quarterlies *Modern Age* and *The University Bookman*. *The Conservative Mind, Edmund Burke, The Roots of American Order, Enemies of the Permanent Things, Eliot and His Age, Rights and Duties, The Politics of Prudence,* and *Redeeming the Time* are among his over thirty books.

Paul Kurtz is Professor Emeritus of Philosophy at the State University of Buffalo. His more recent works include *The Courage to Become: The Virtues of Humanism* and *Towards a New Enlightenment*.

Tibor R. Machan is Distinguished Fellow and Professor at the Leatherby Center for Entrepreneurship and Business Ethics, Chapman University. His most recent work is *A Primer on Ethics*.

Edward B. McLean is the Eugene N. and Marian C. Beesley Chair in Political Science at Wabash College. He holds a J.D. and Ph.D. from Indiana University and has recently published *Law and Civilization: The Legal Thought of Roscoe Pound.*

Frank S. Meyer (1909-1972) was one of the original senior editors of *National Review.* He wrote and edited several works, the most notable being *In Defense of Freedom: A Conservative Credo.*

Robert Nisbet (1913-1996) taught Sociology at Columbia University and the University of California, Berkeley, and was Adjunct Scholar at the American Enterprise Institute. He authored several books including *The Quest for Community* and *Twilight of Authority.*

Murray N. Rothbard (1926-1995) was S. J. Hall Distinguished Professor of Economics at the University of Nevada, Las Vegas, at the time of his death. He was one of the founders of the Libertarian Party and the author of several works including *The Libertarian Manifesto* and *Man, Economy and State.*

Richard M. Weaver (1910-1963) was Professor of English at the University of Chicago from 1945 until his death. The best known of his works are *Ideas Have Consequences, Visions of Order,* and *The Ethics of Rhetoric.*

Frederick D. Wilhelmsen (1923-1996) was Professor of Philosophy and Politics at the University of Dallas. He was the author of numerous works, among them *Christianity and Political Philosophy, Being and Knowing,* and *The Paradoxical Structure of Existence.*